To thank God, who gives us health and wisdom every day. I dedicate this work to you, my son, who fills me with motivation, love and the strength to win.
I love you P.F

Mente Inteligente P.D®
2024

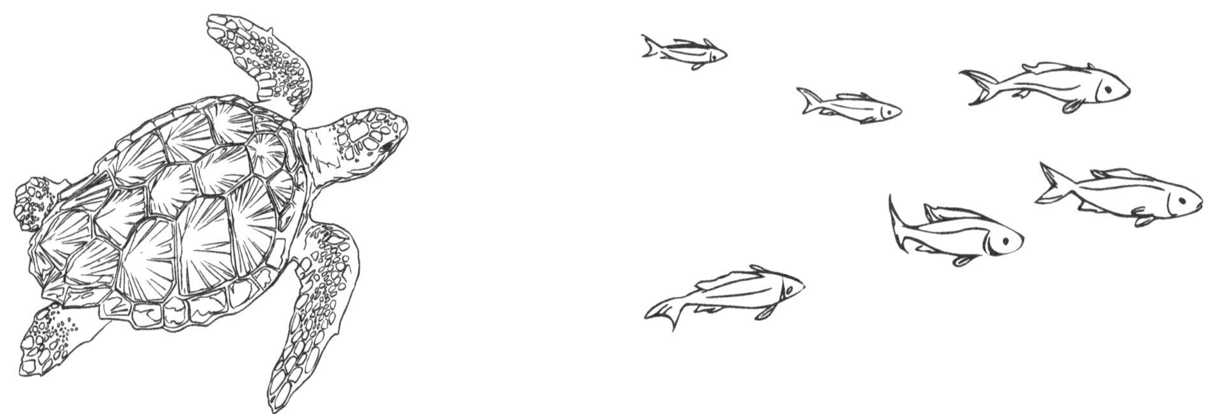

This Book Belongs to:

....

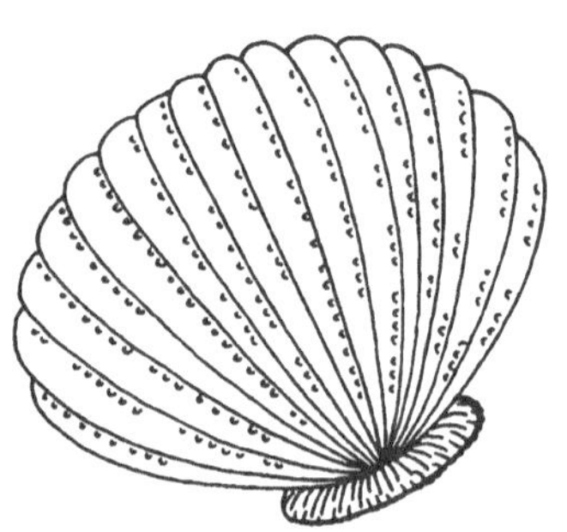

Test Color Page

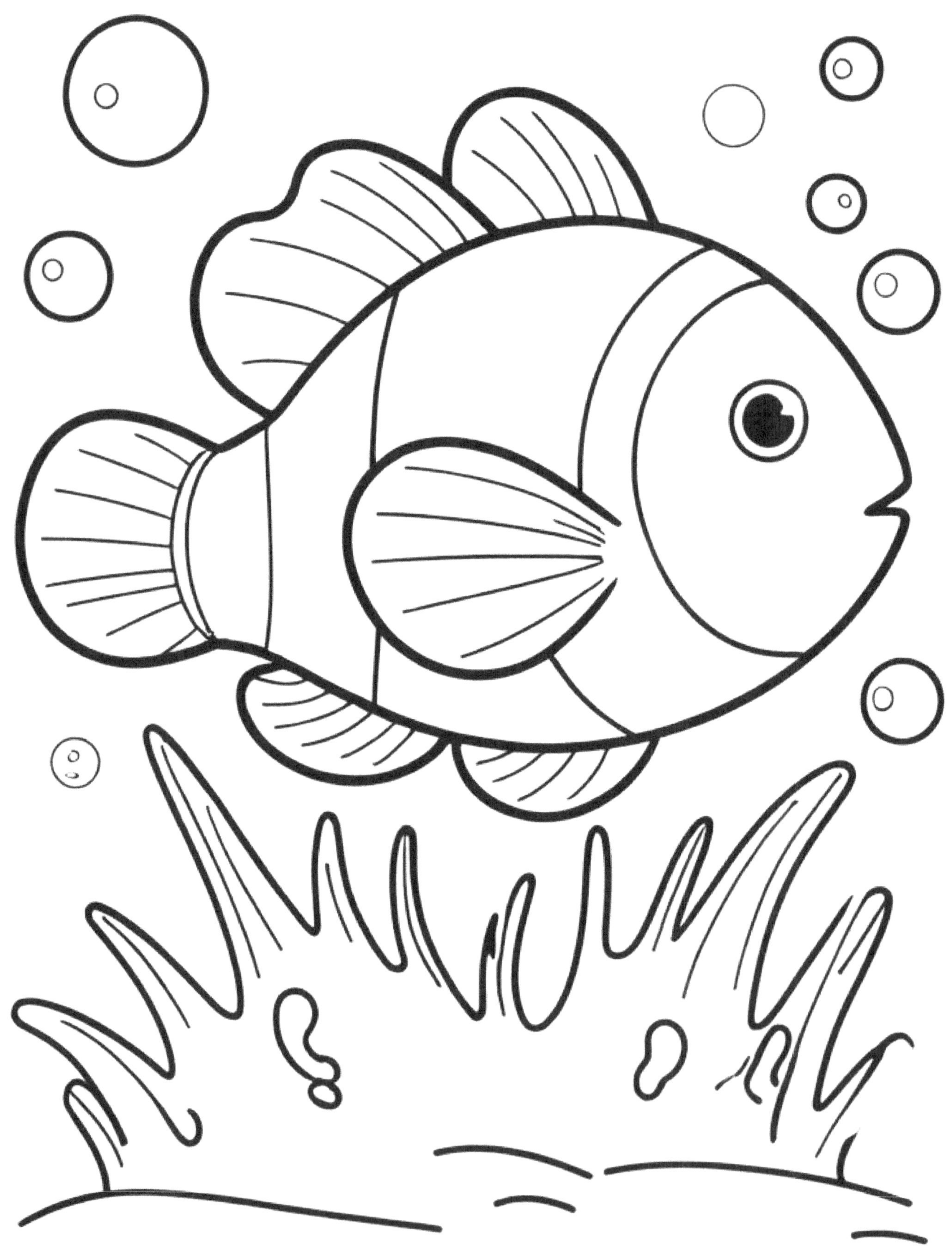

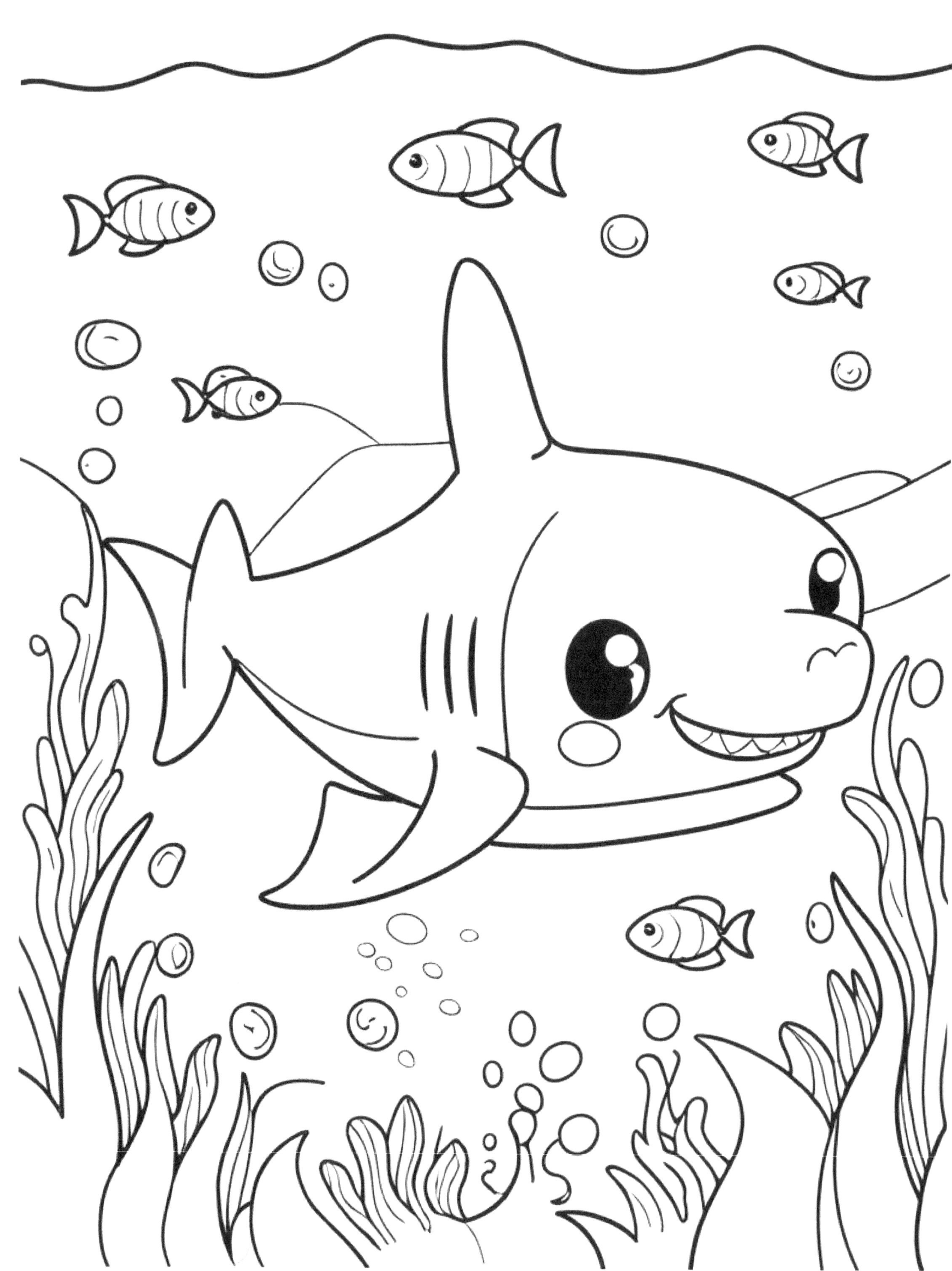

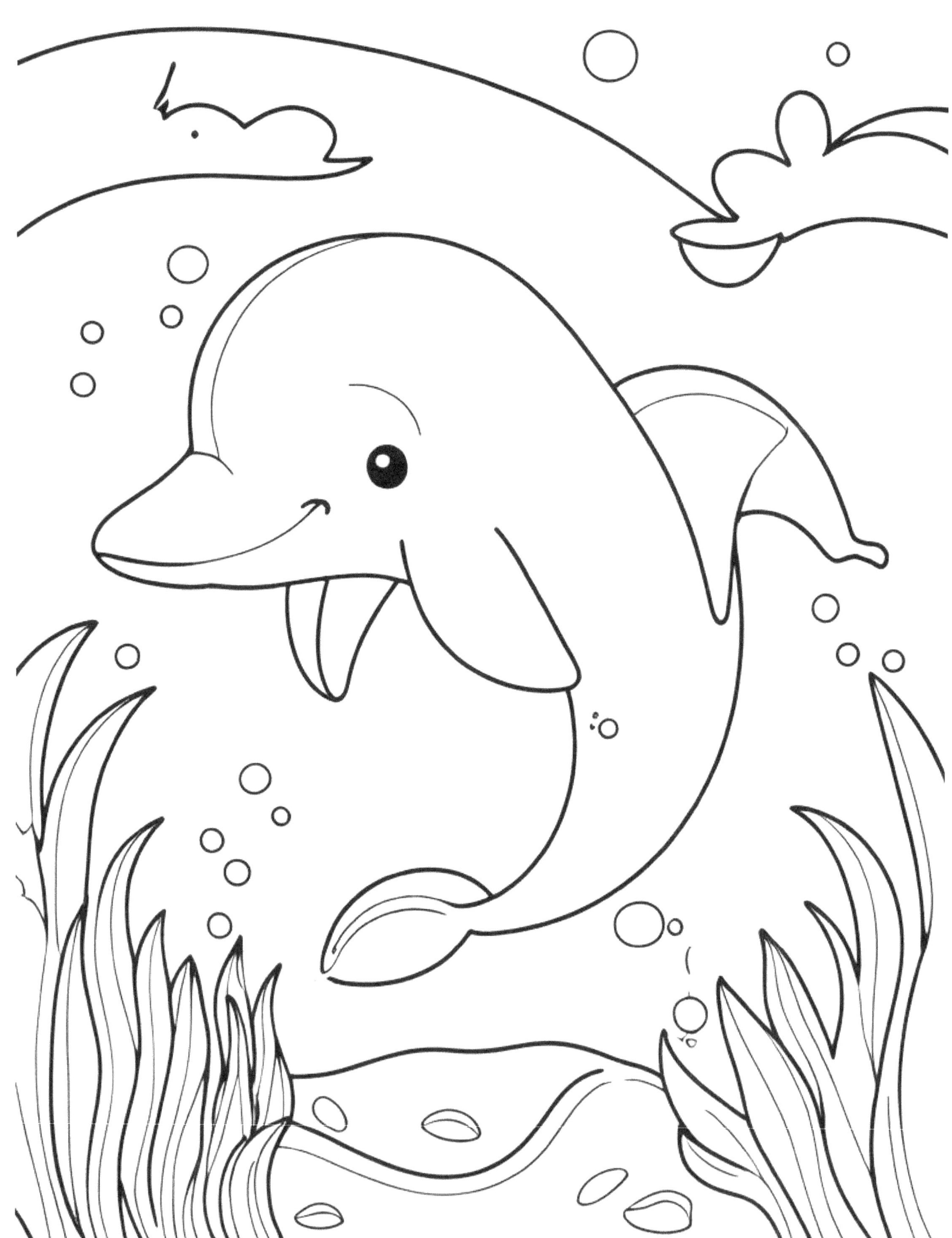

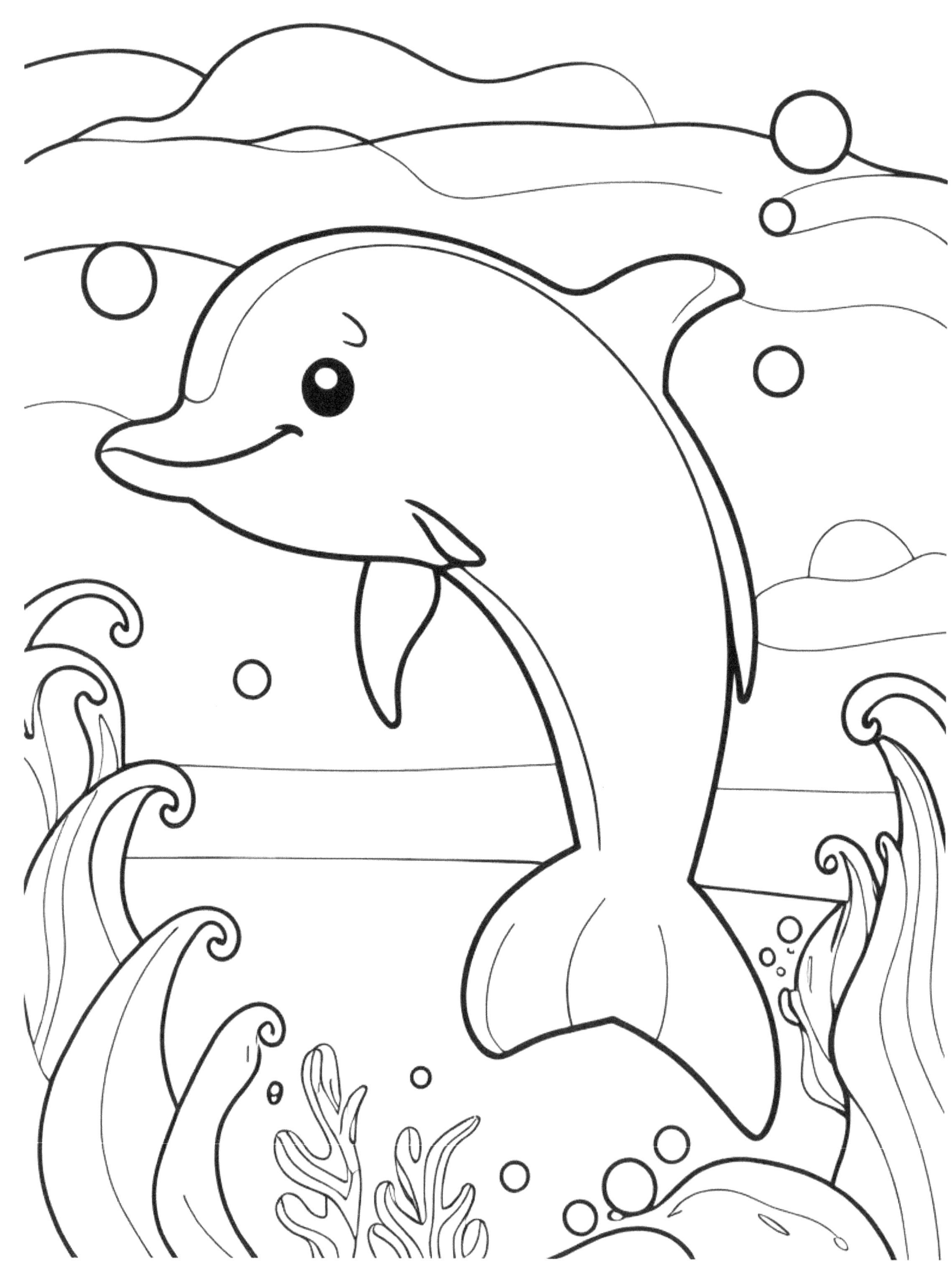

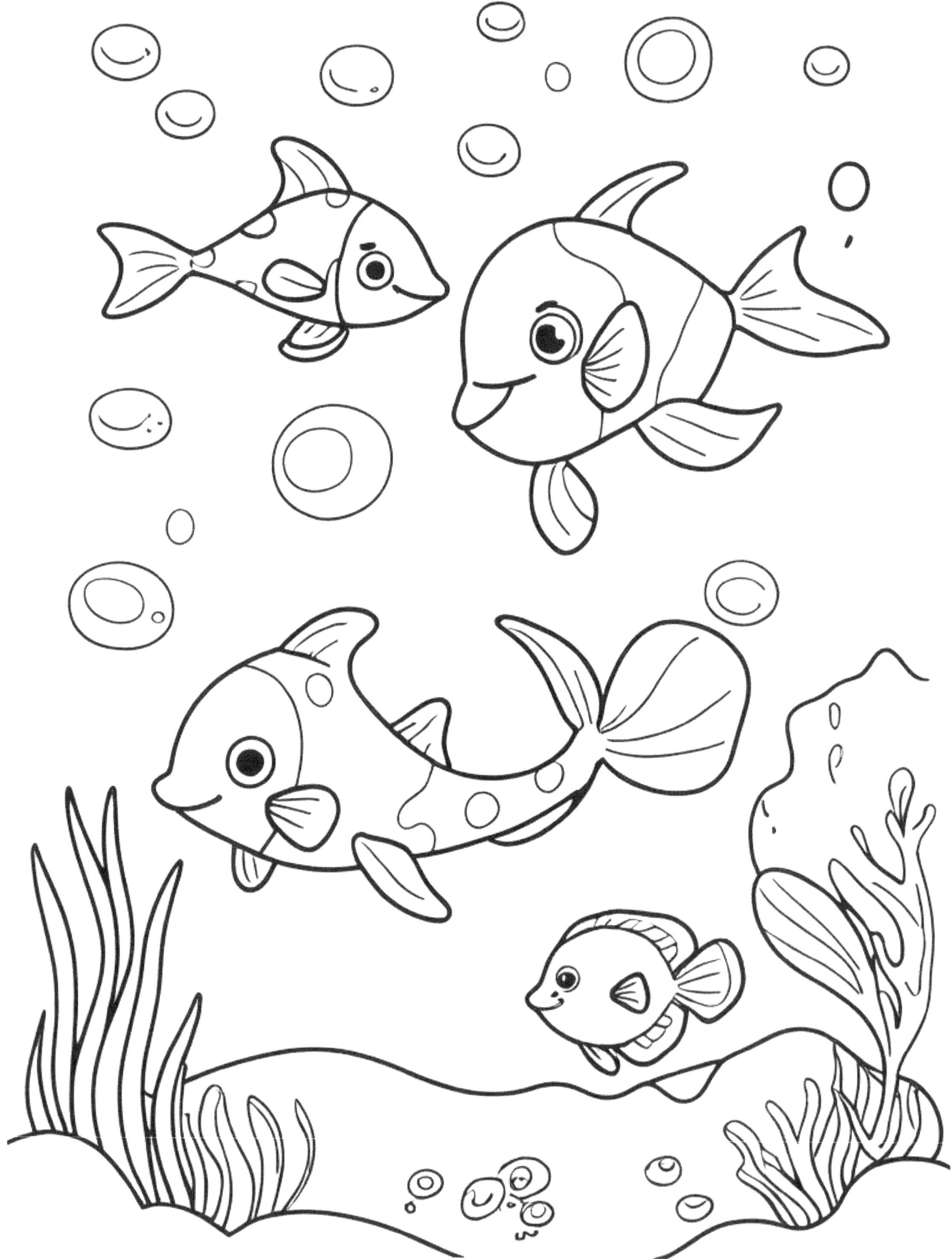

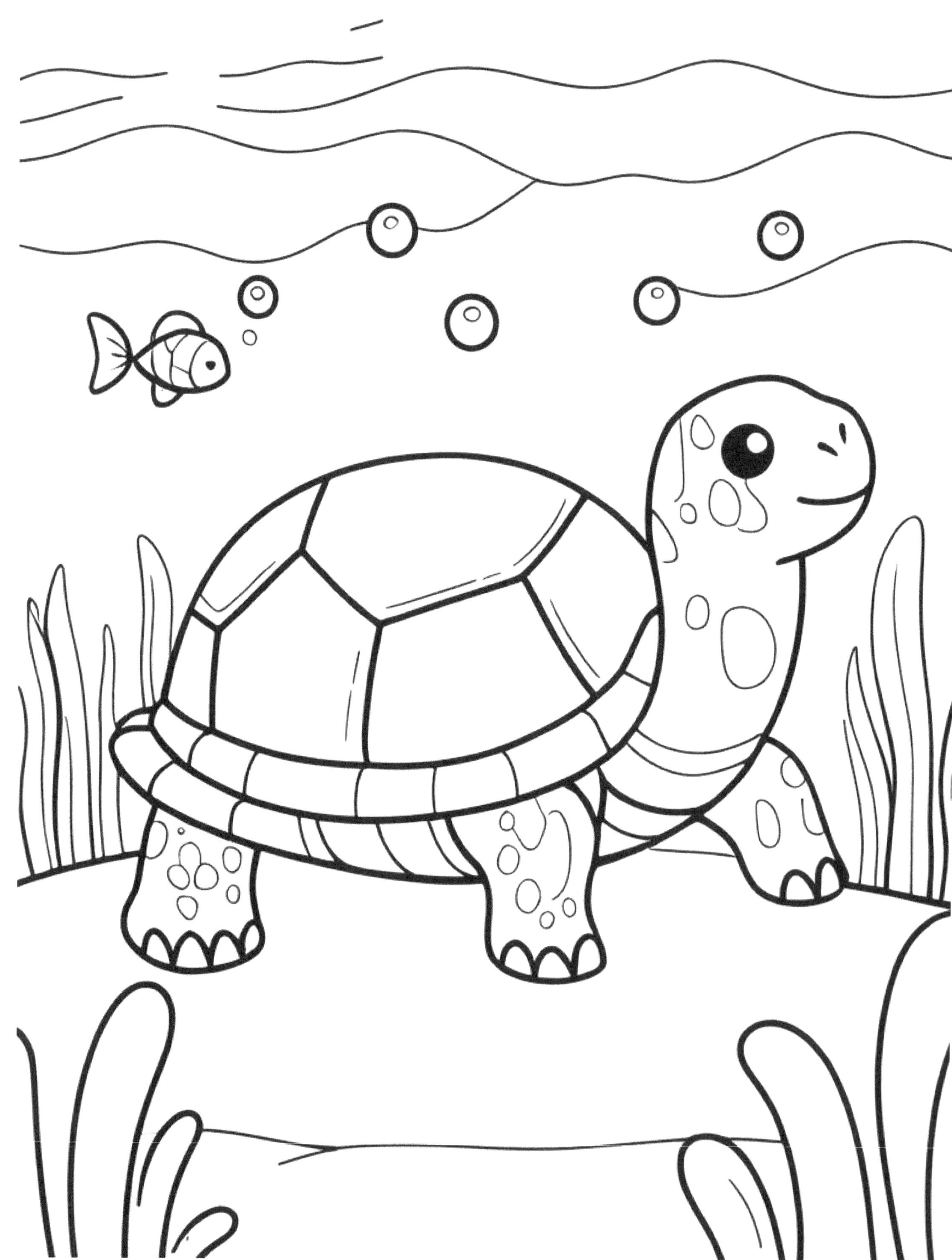

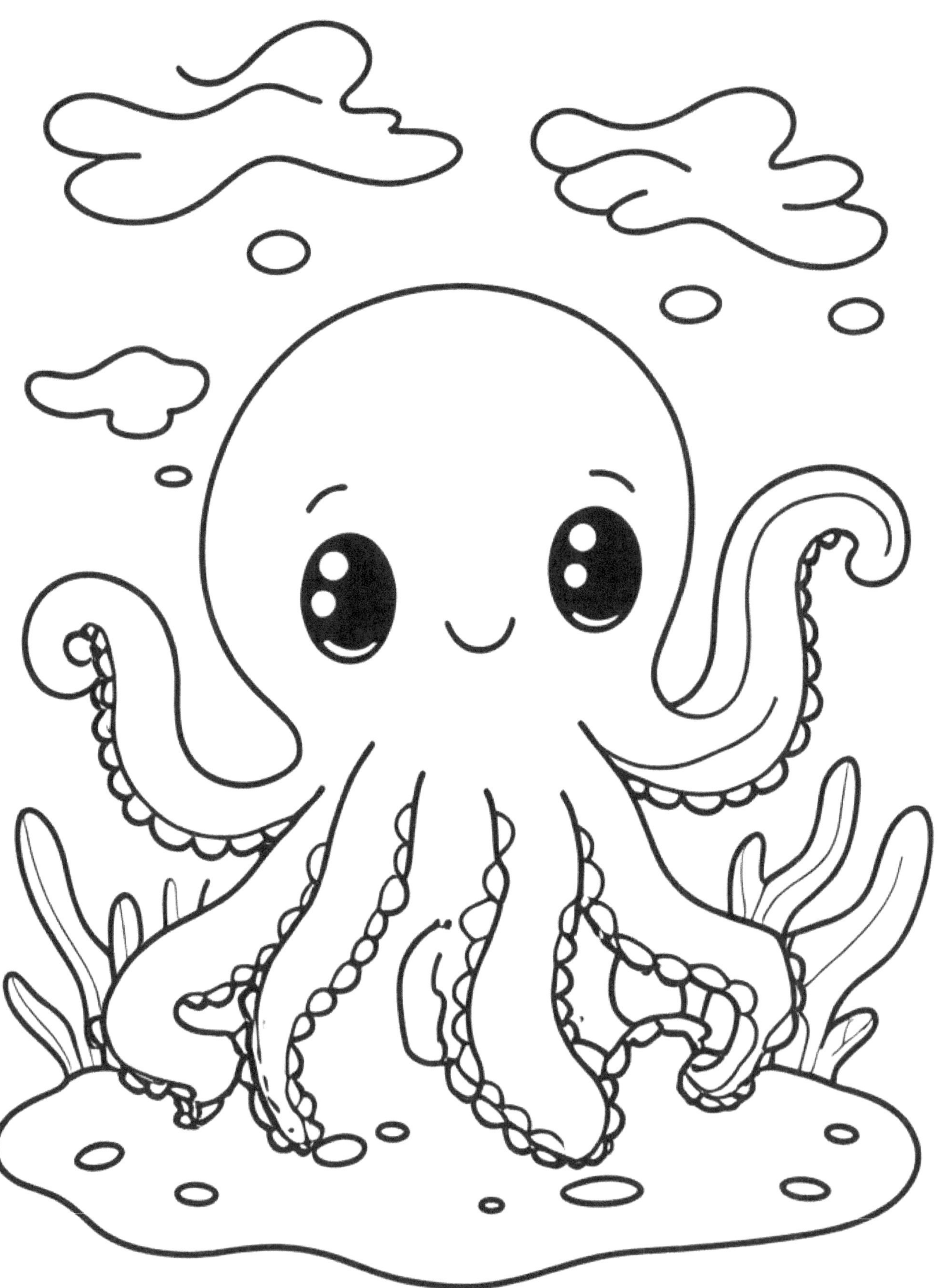

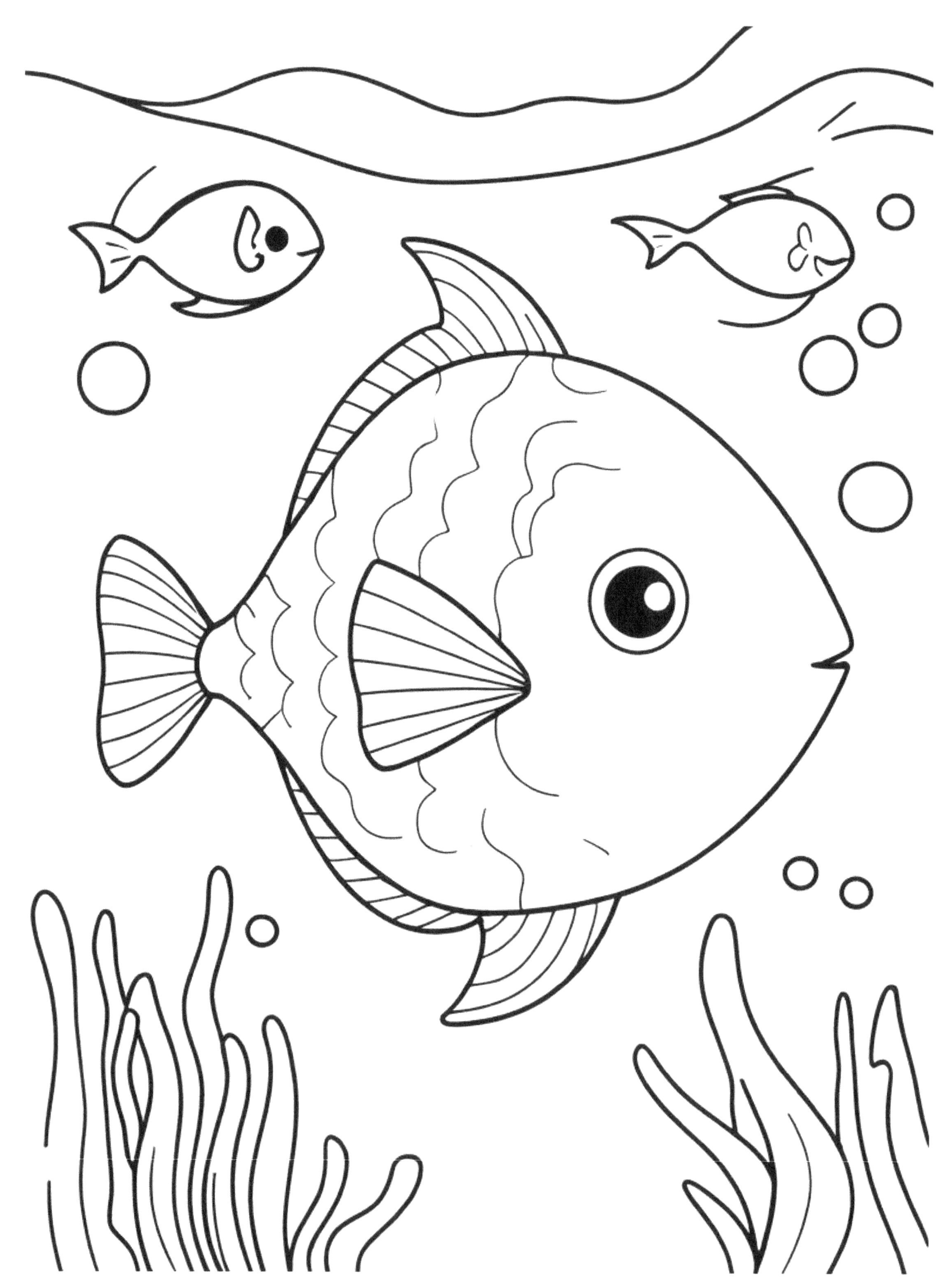

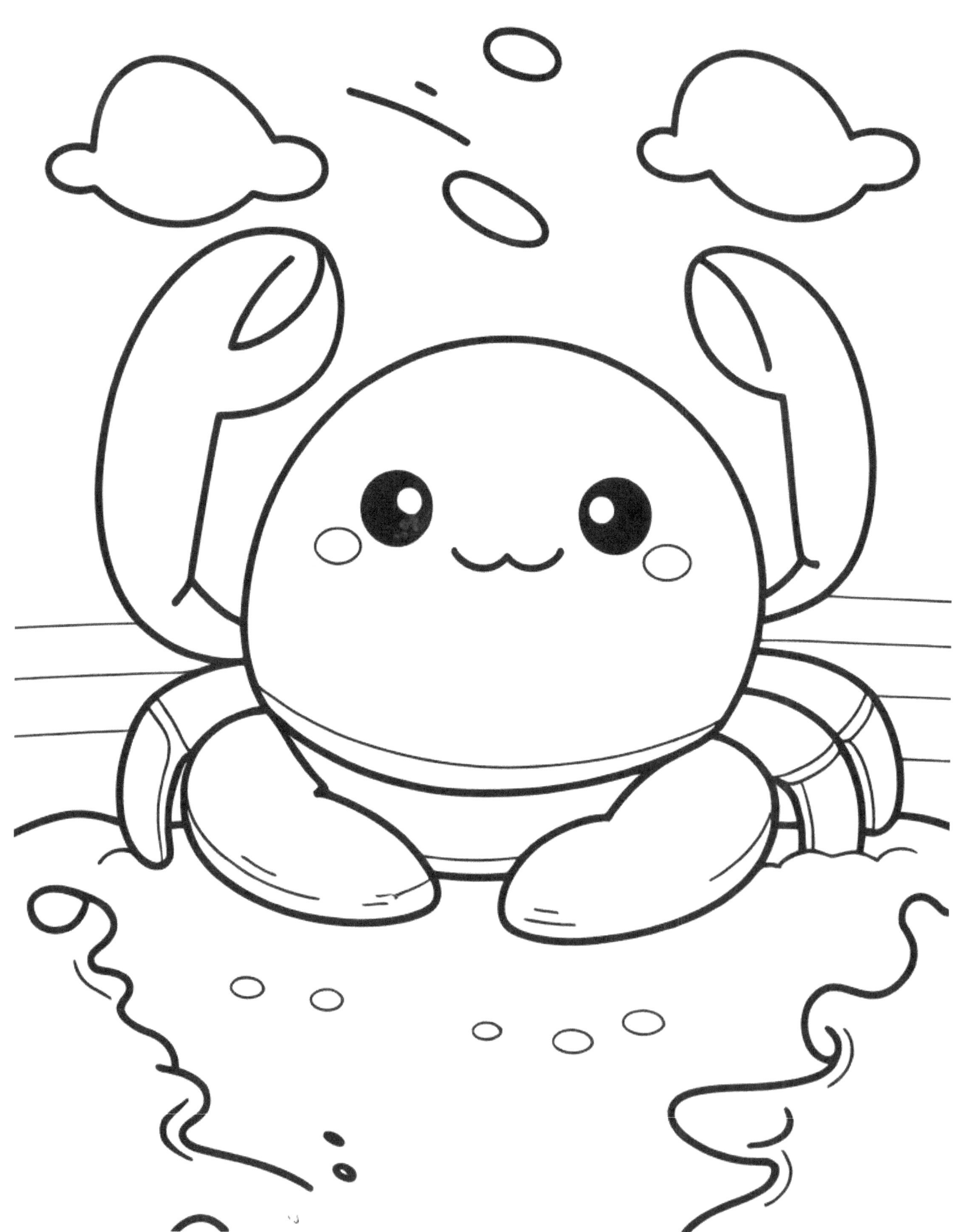

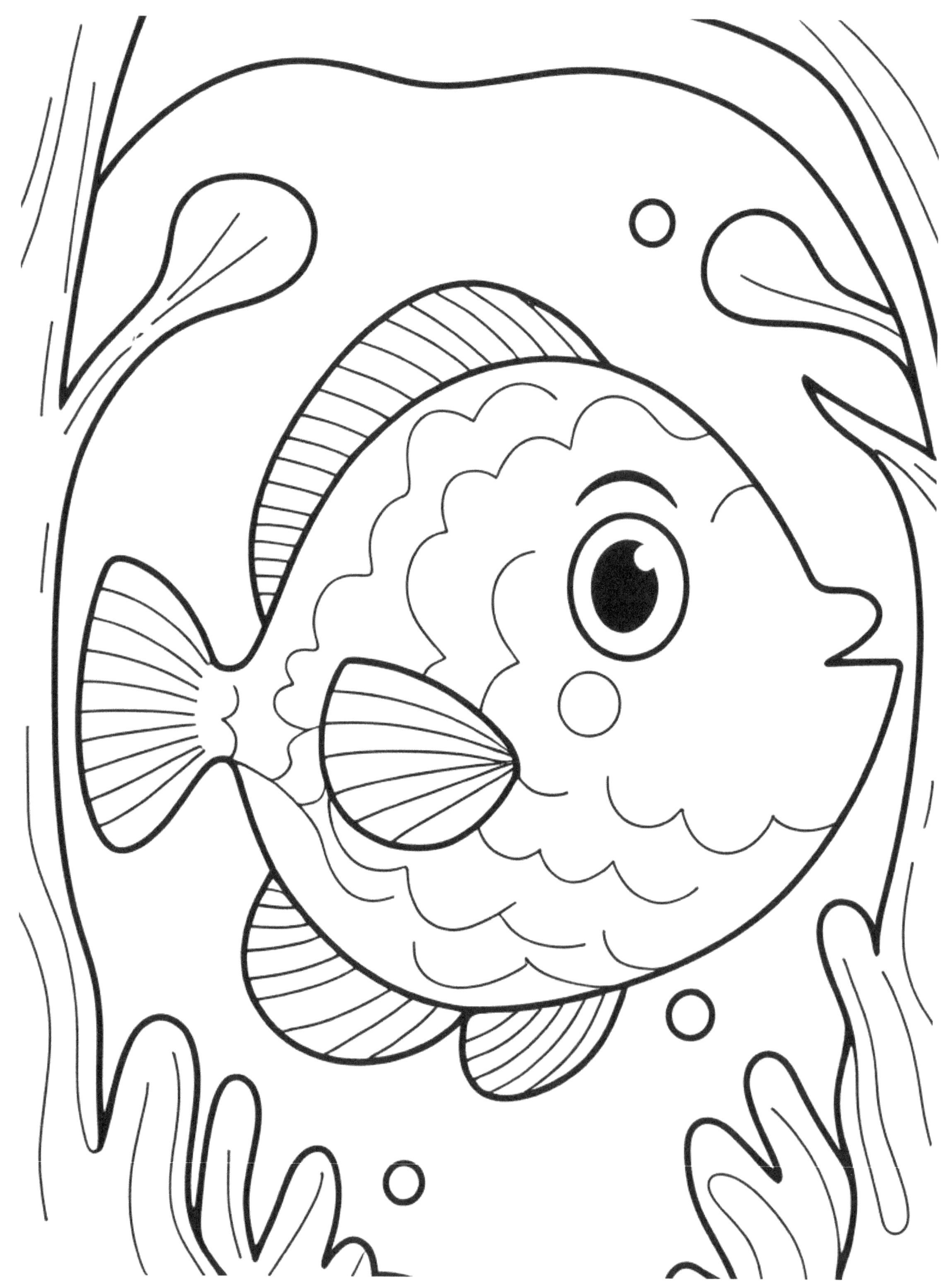

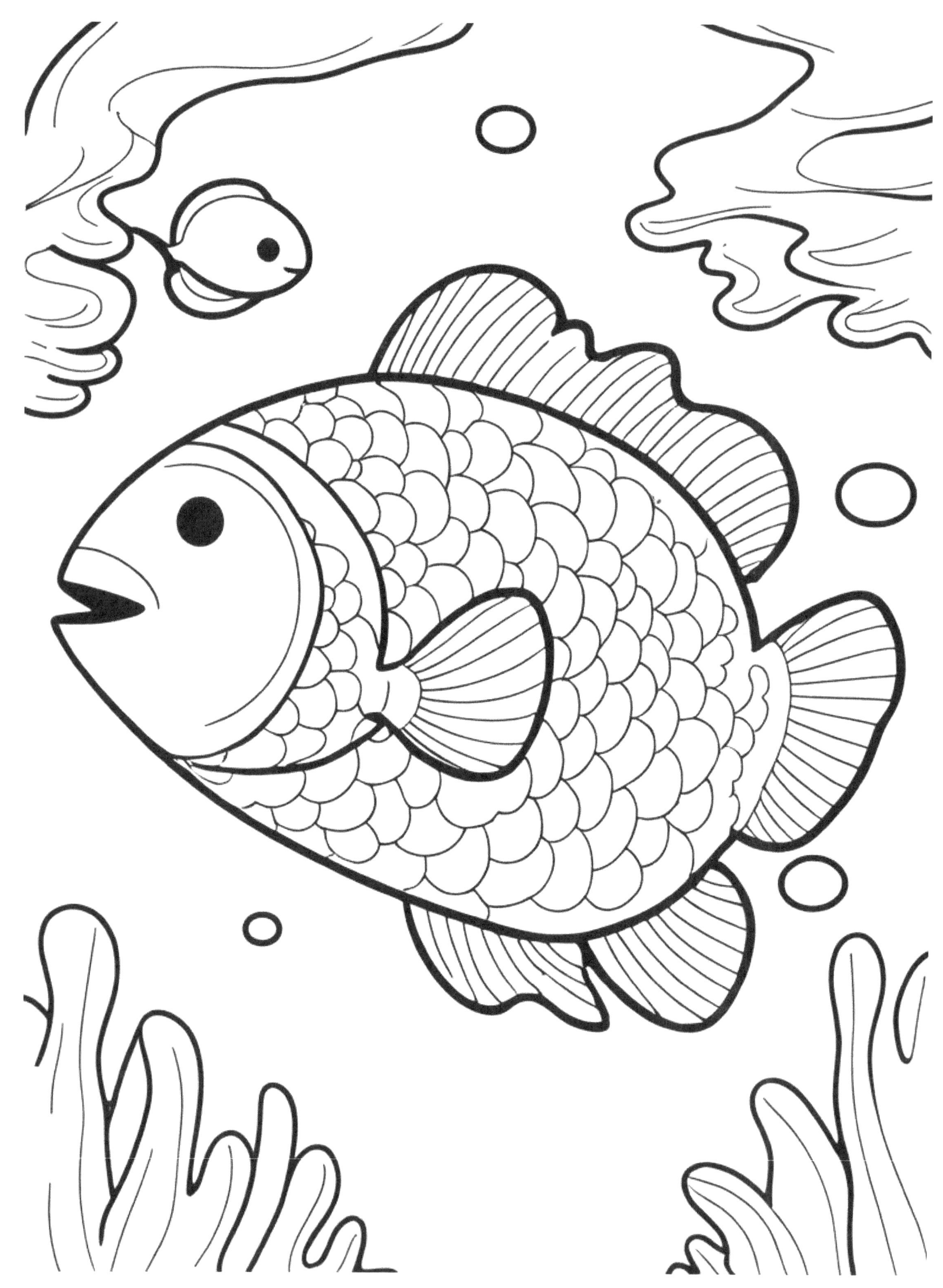

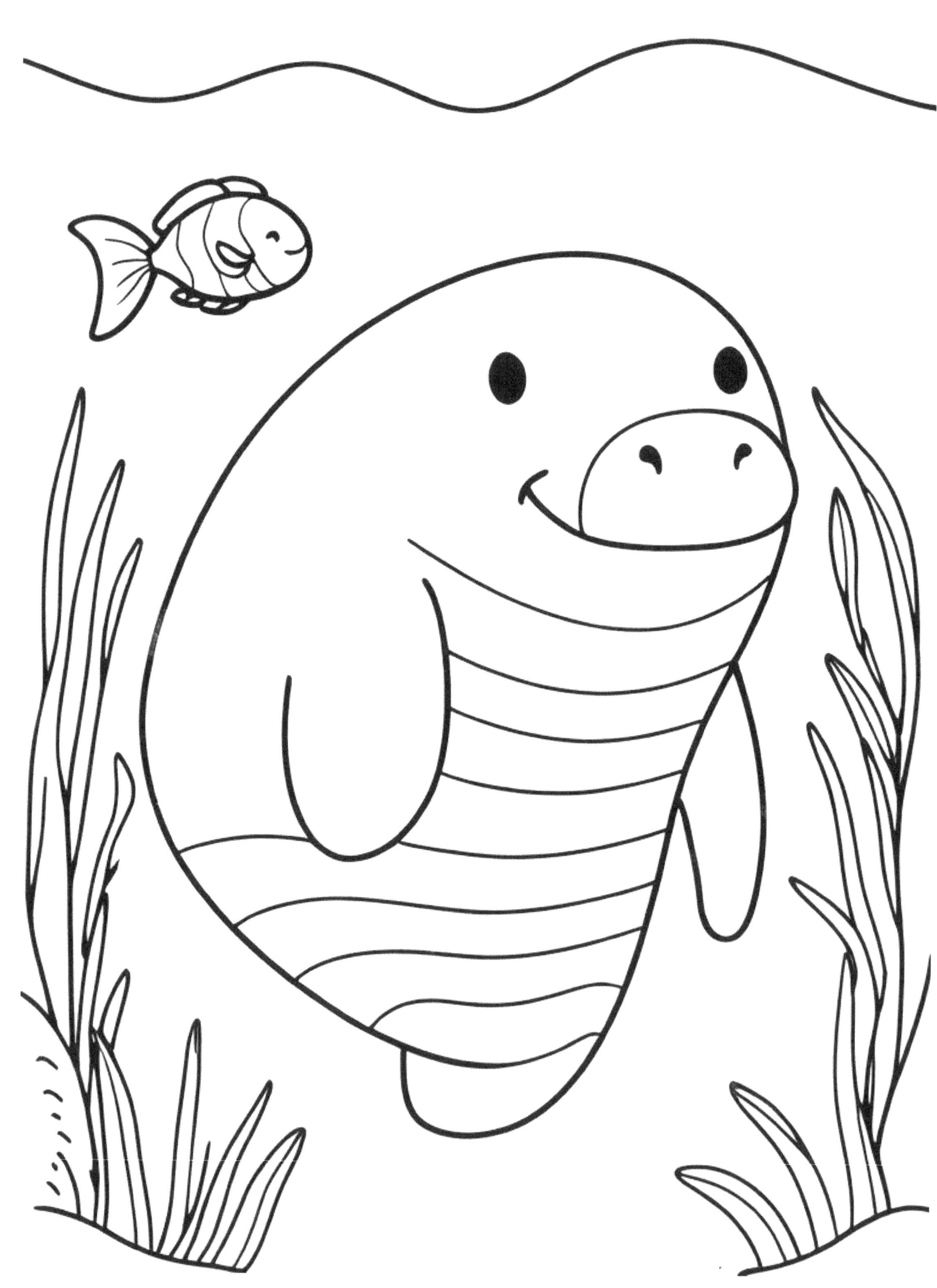

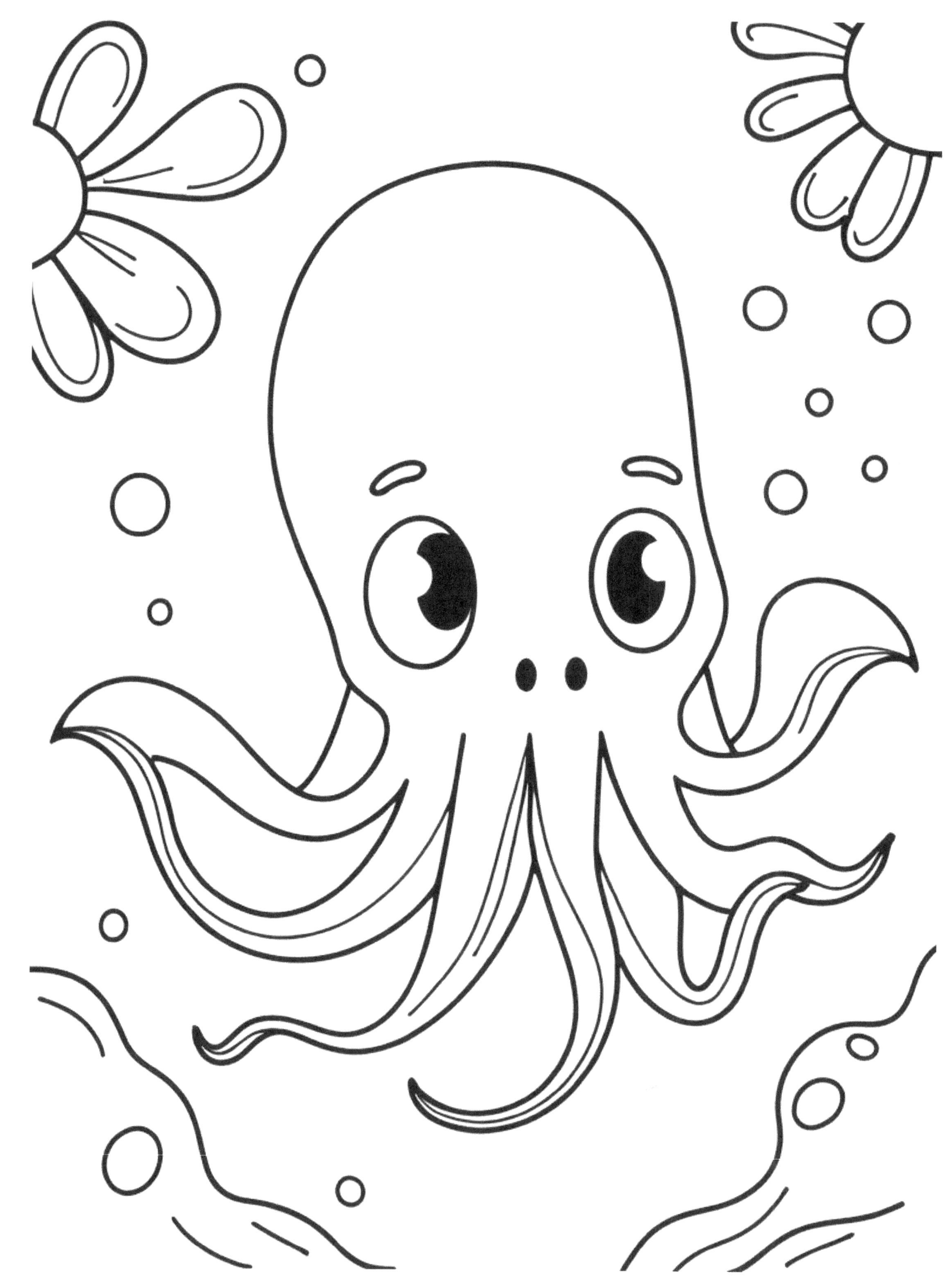

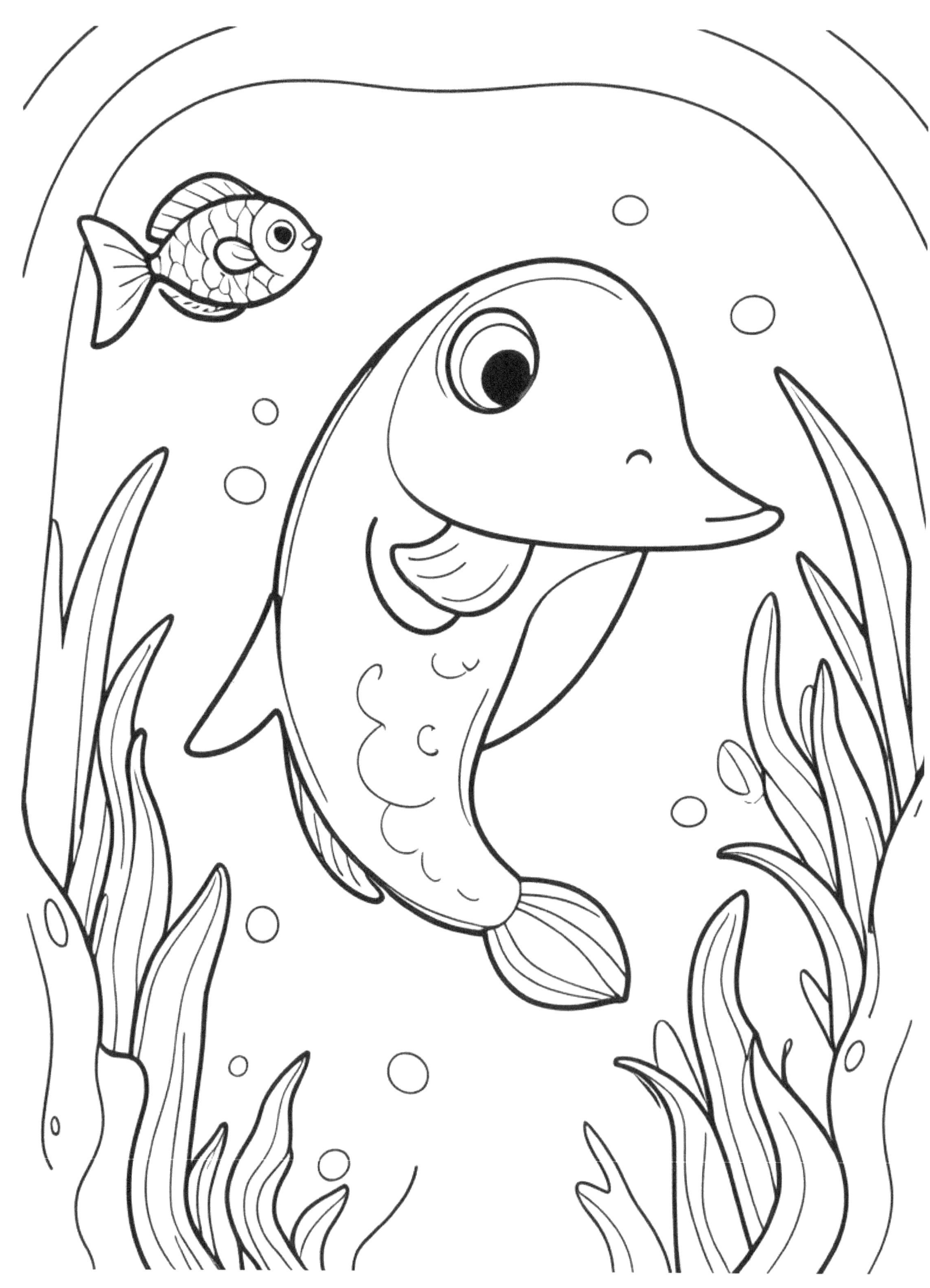

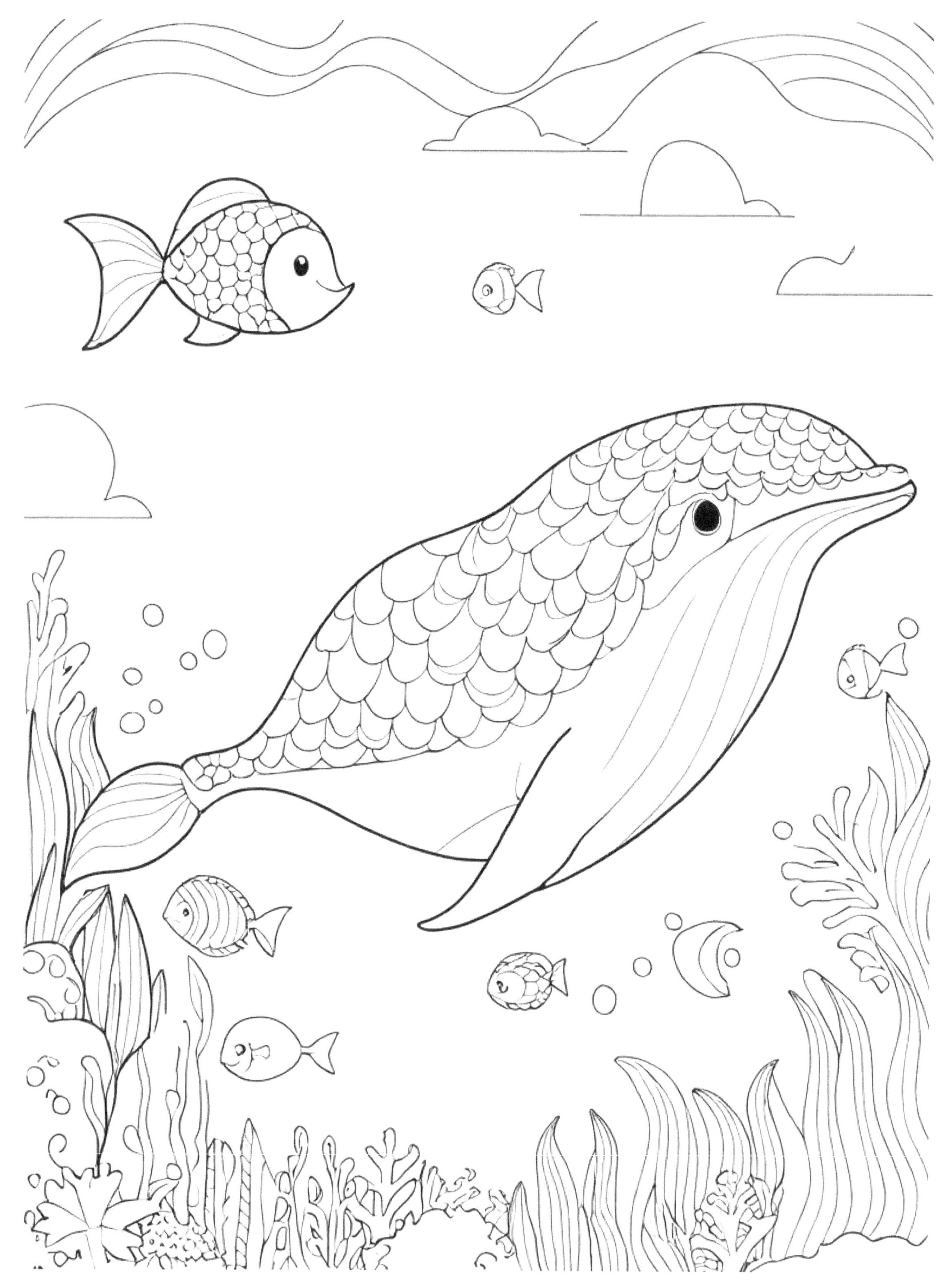

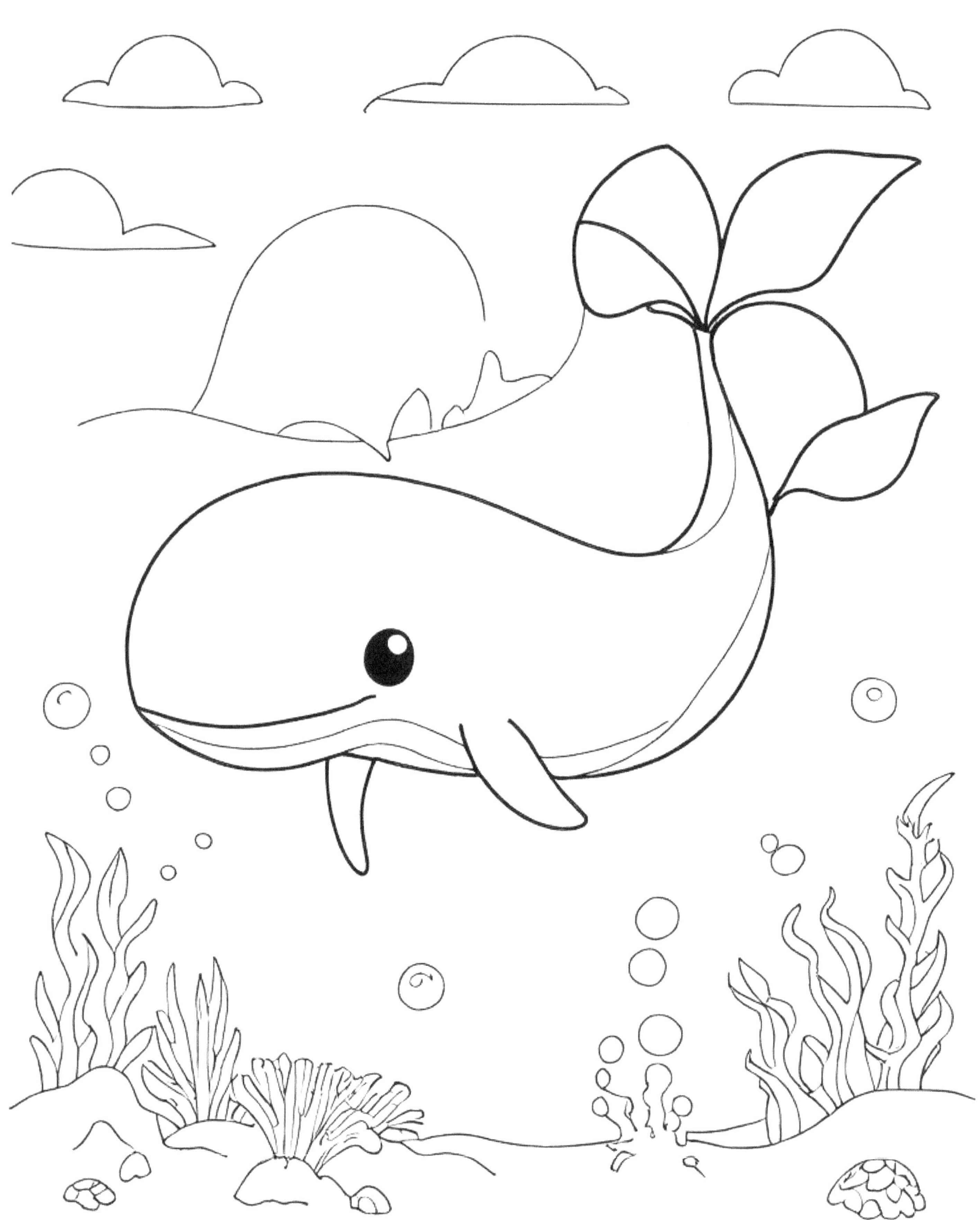

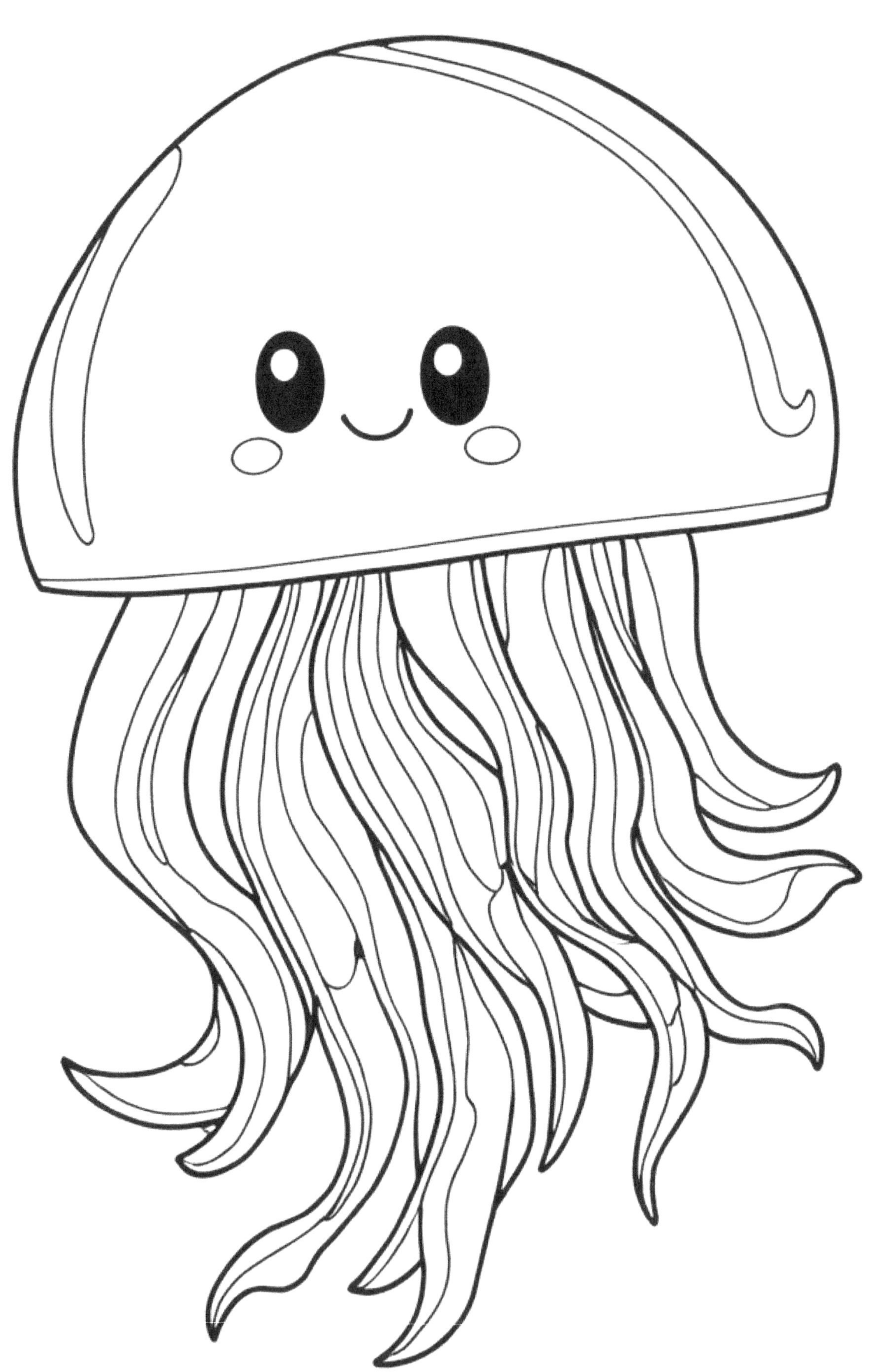

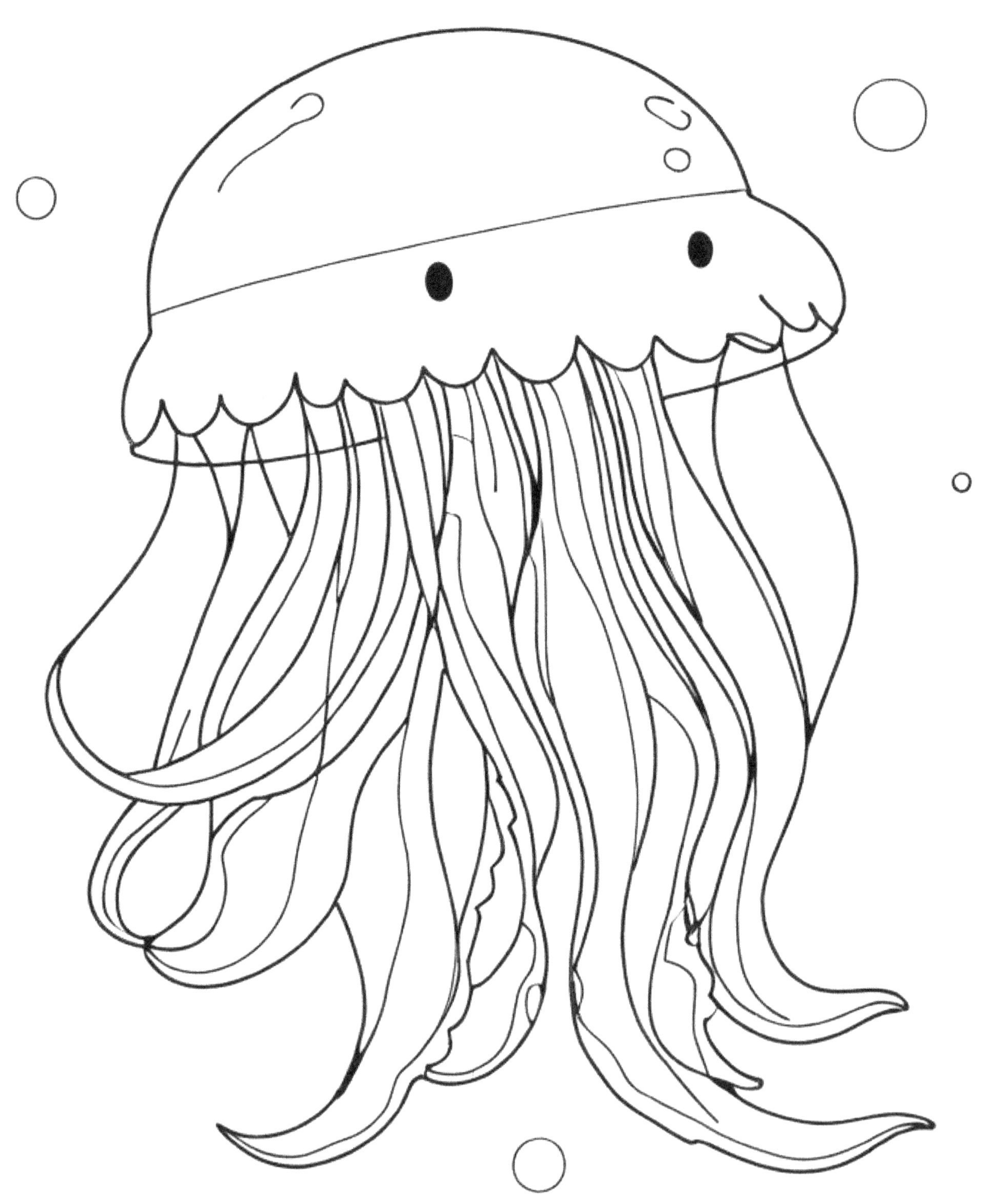

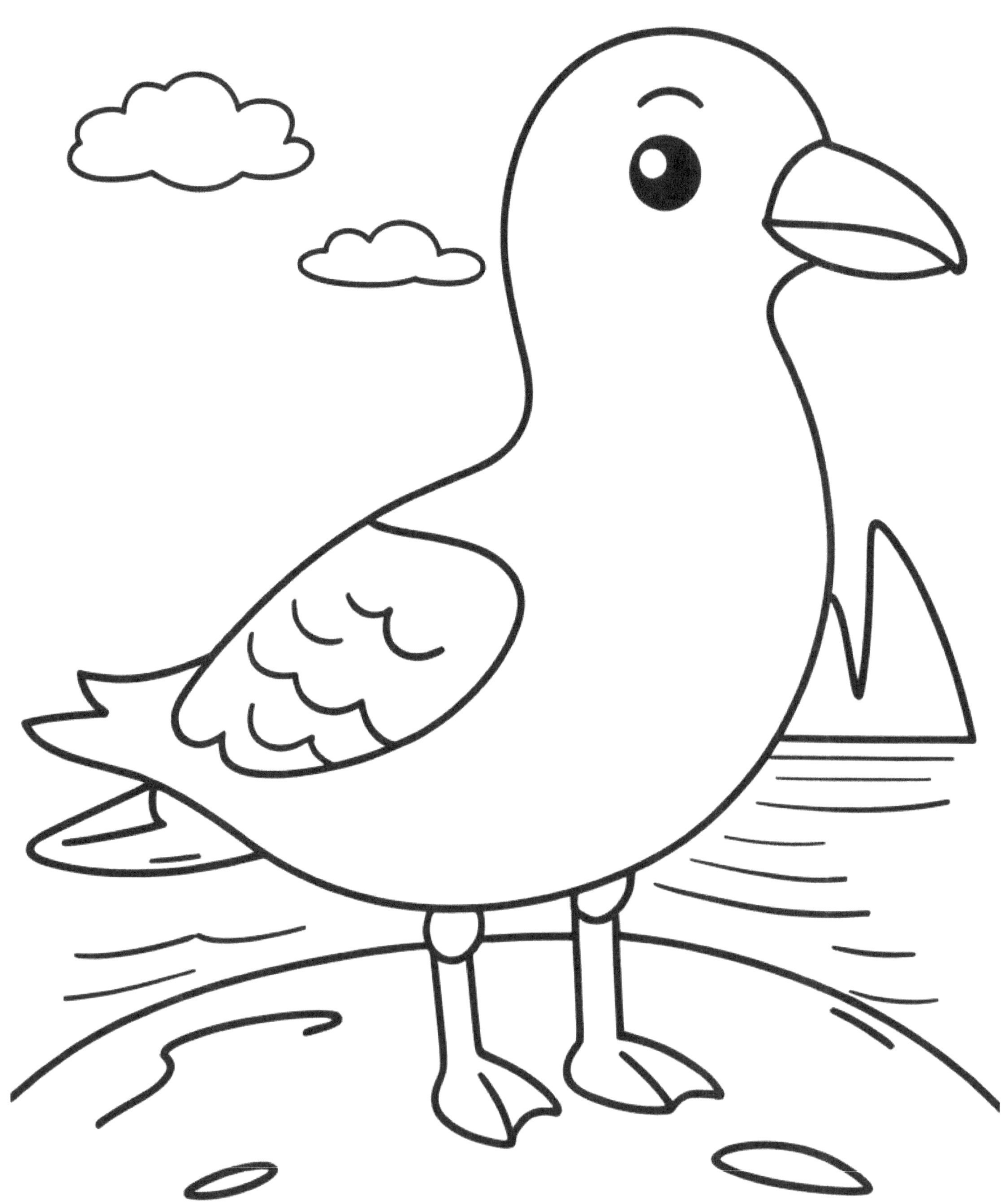

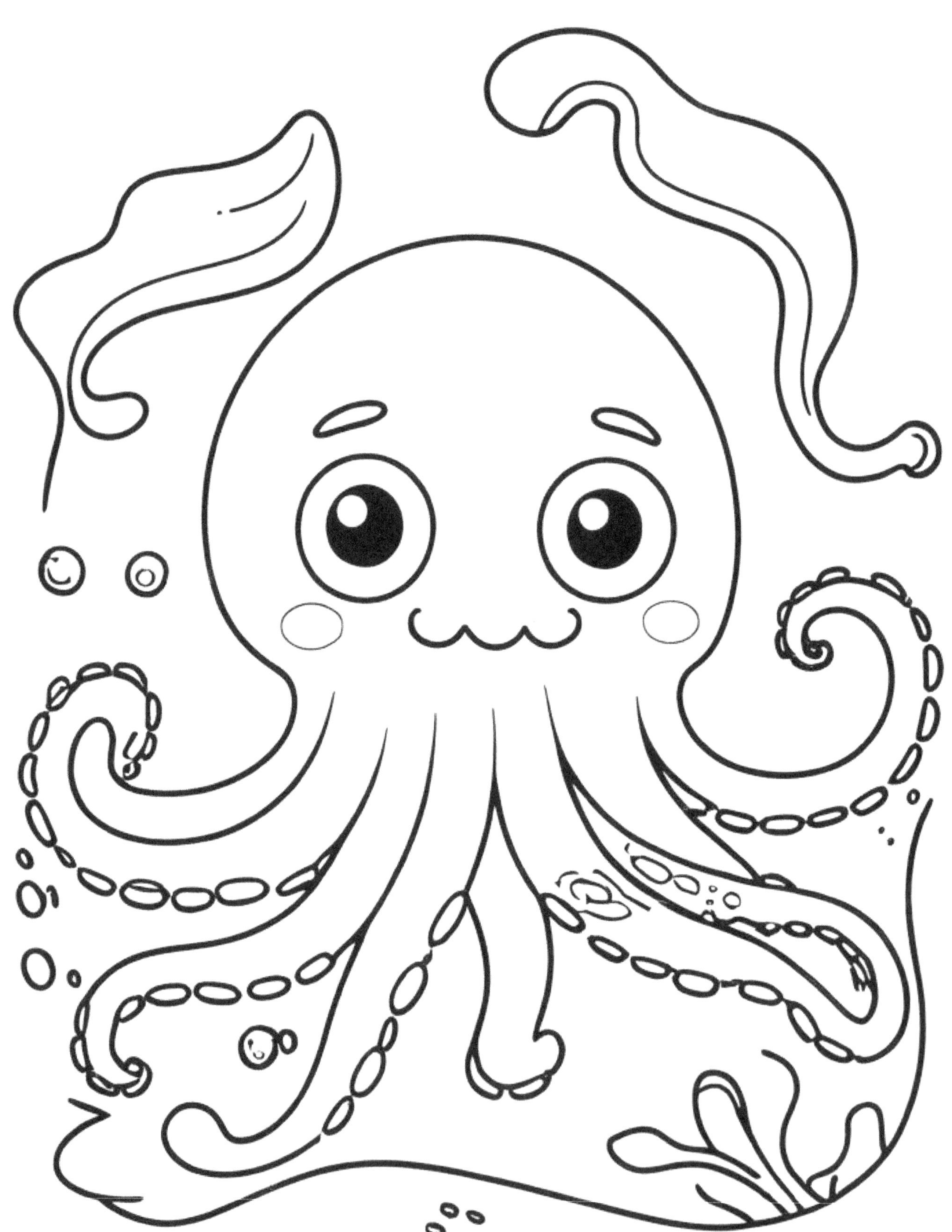

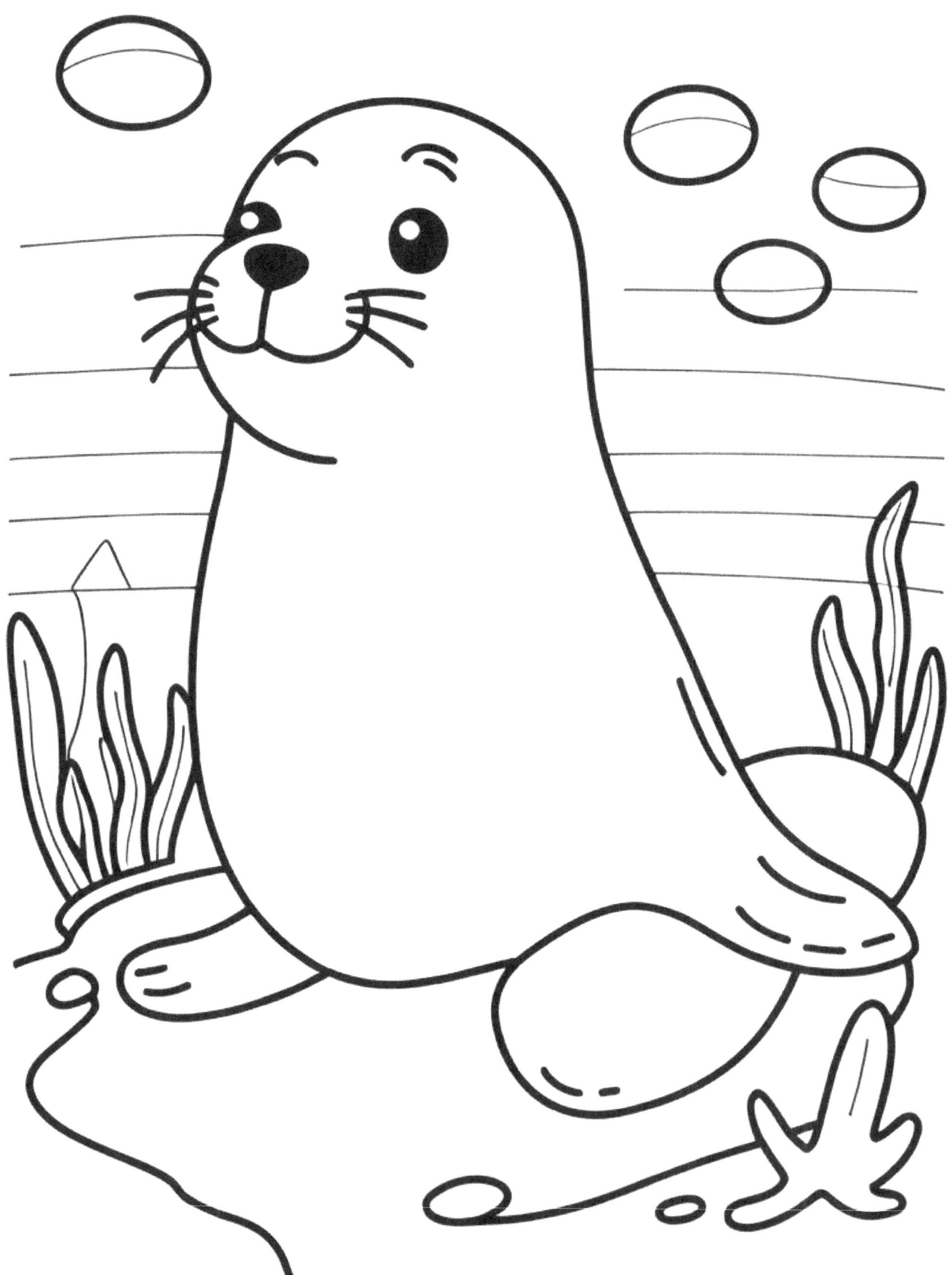

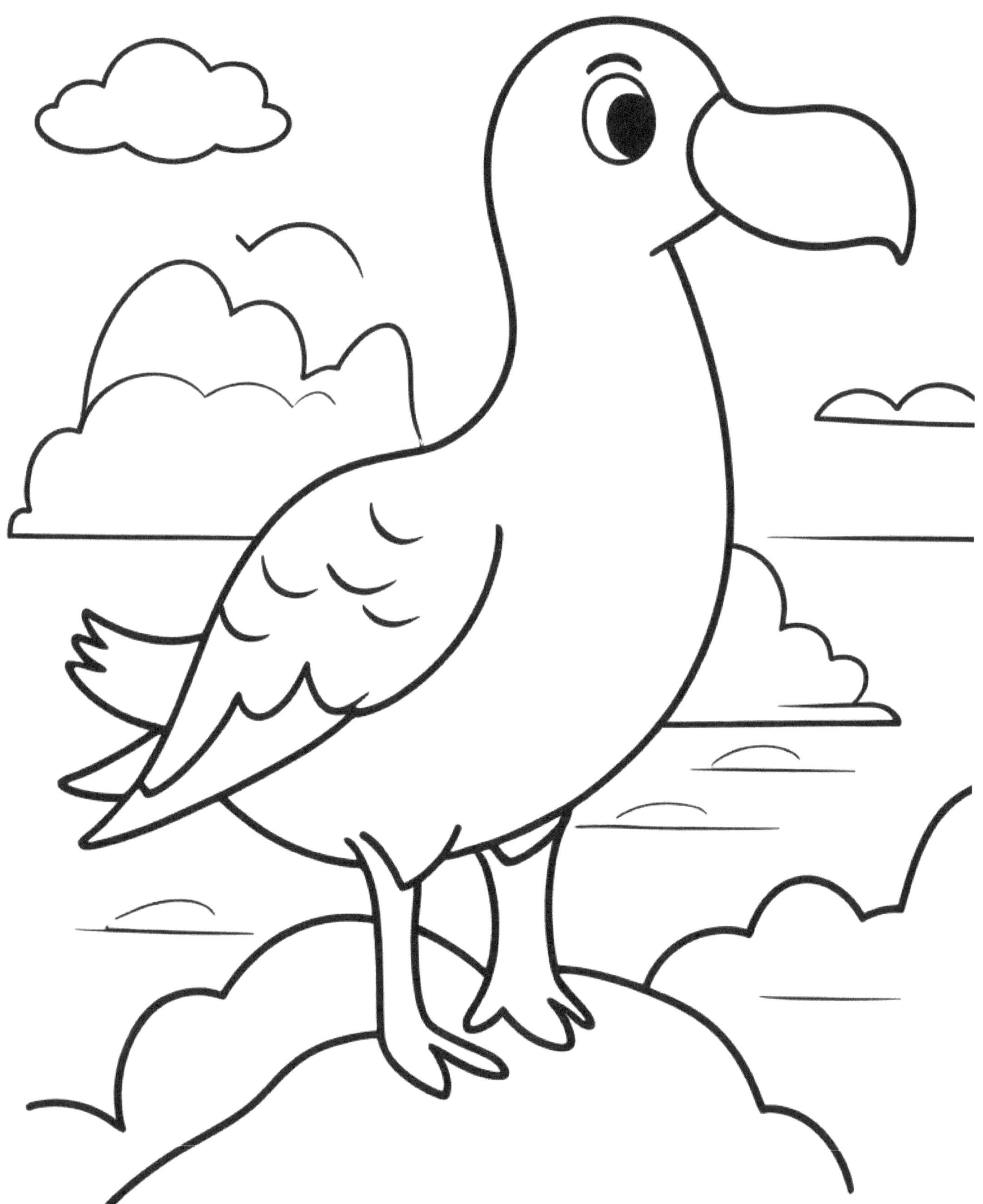

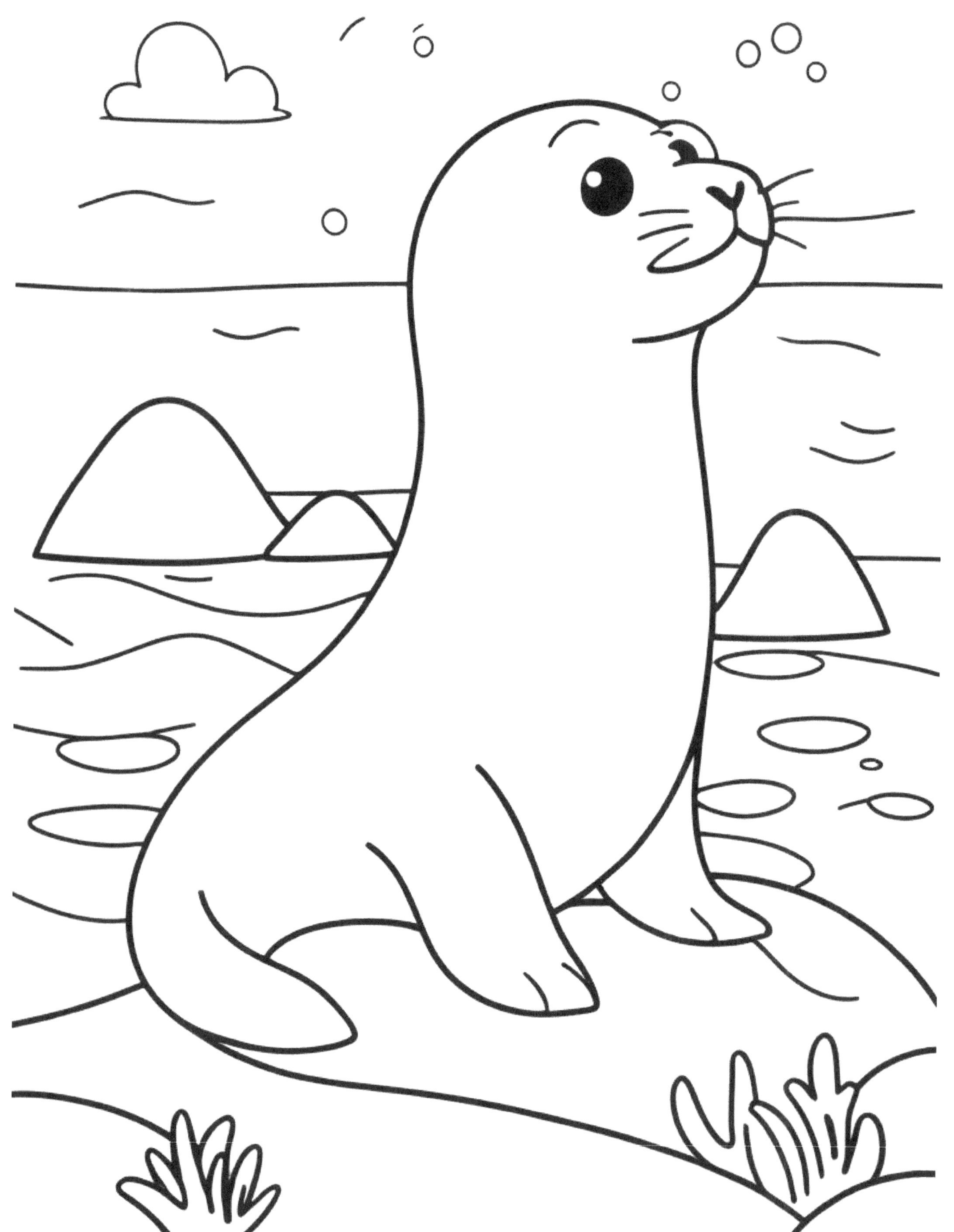

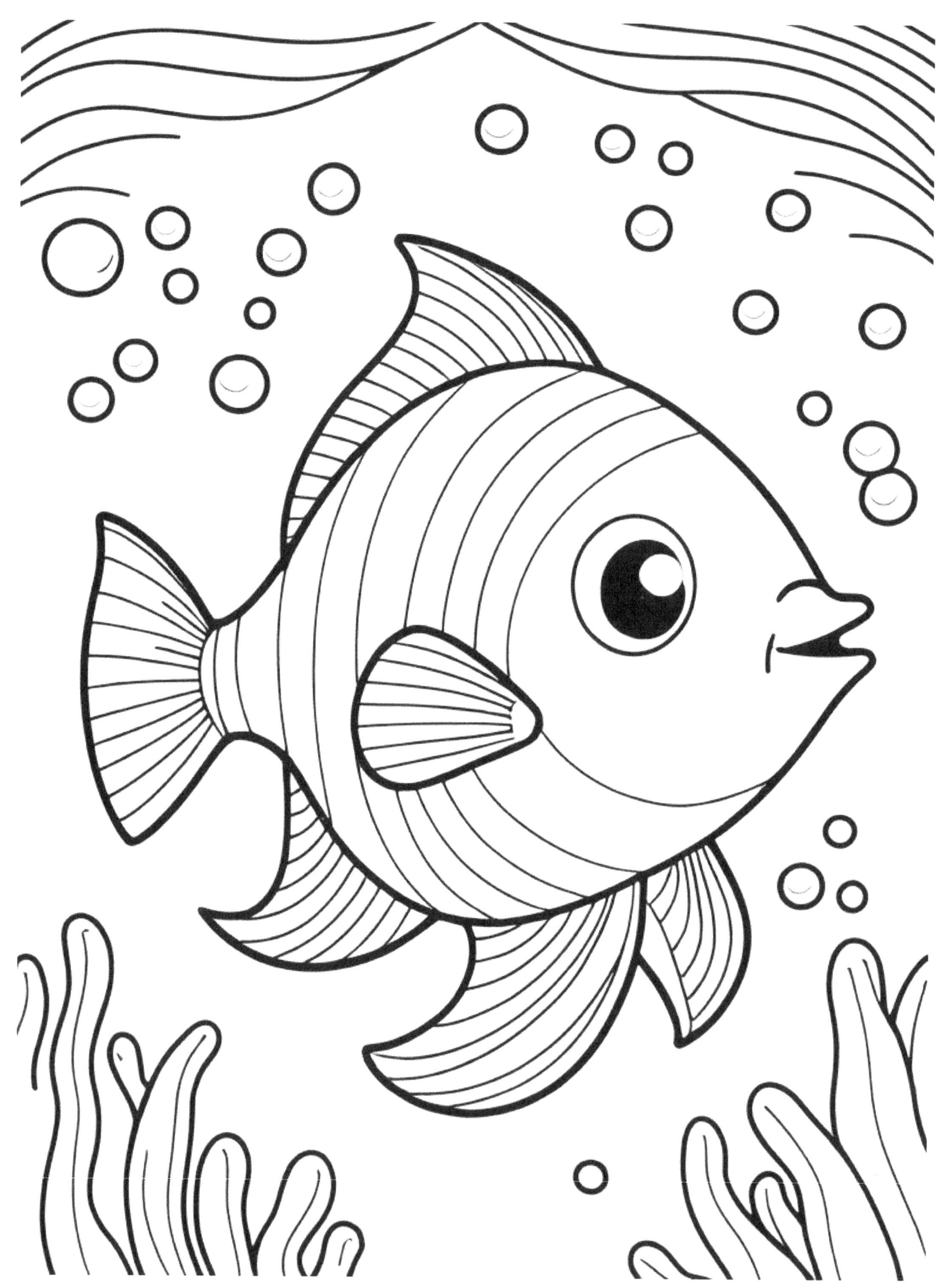

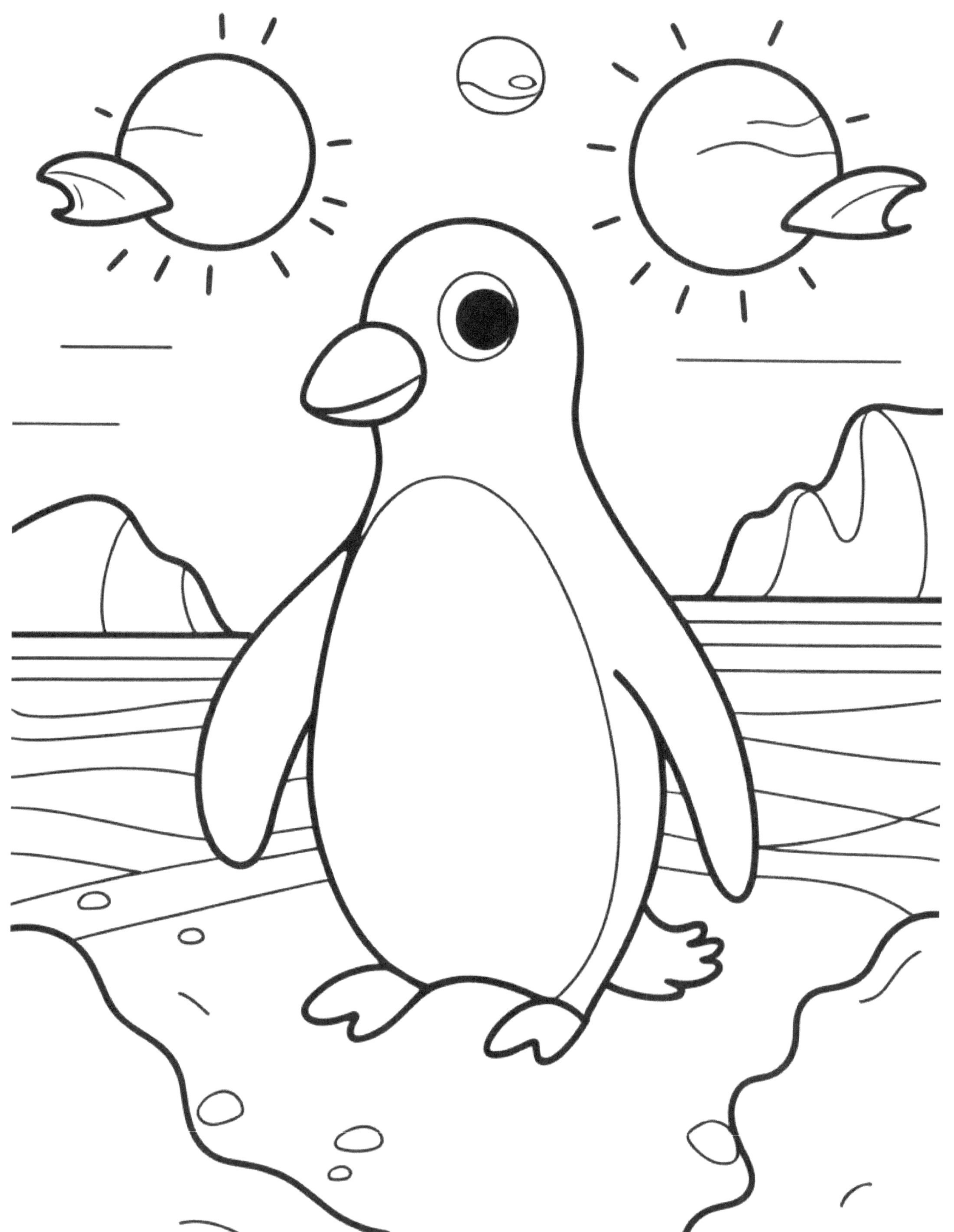

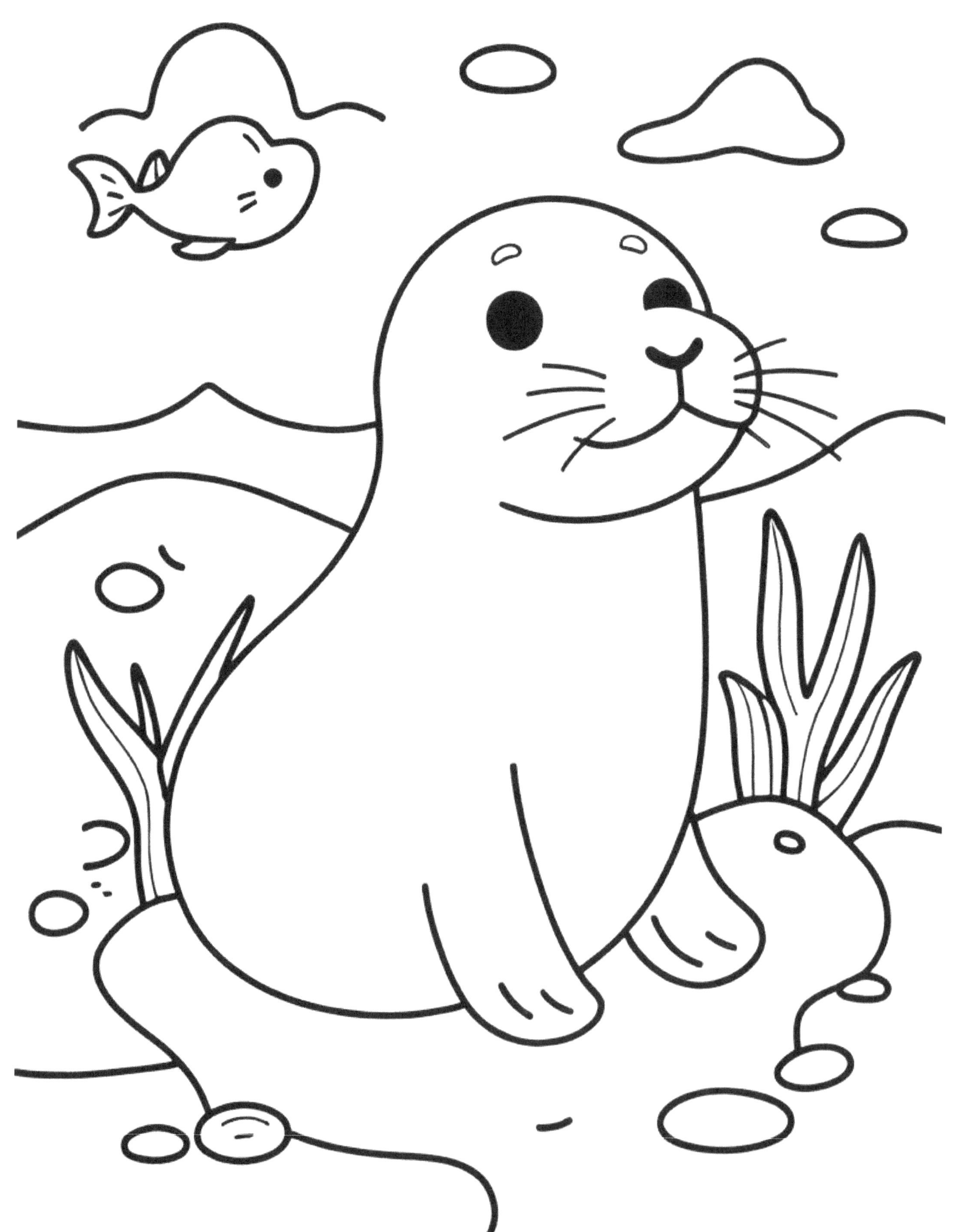

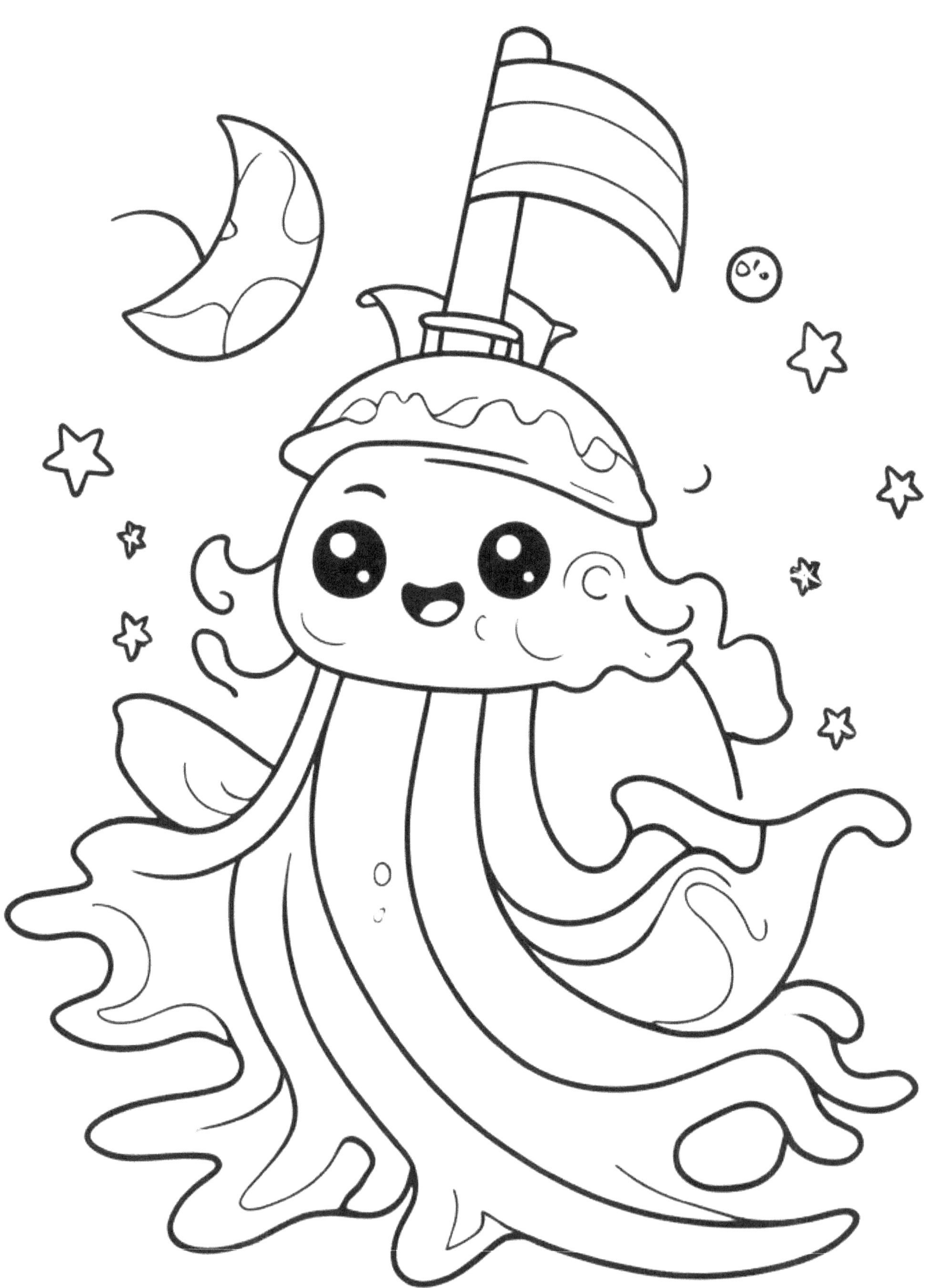

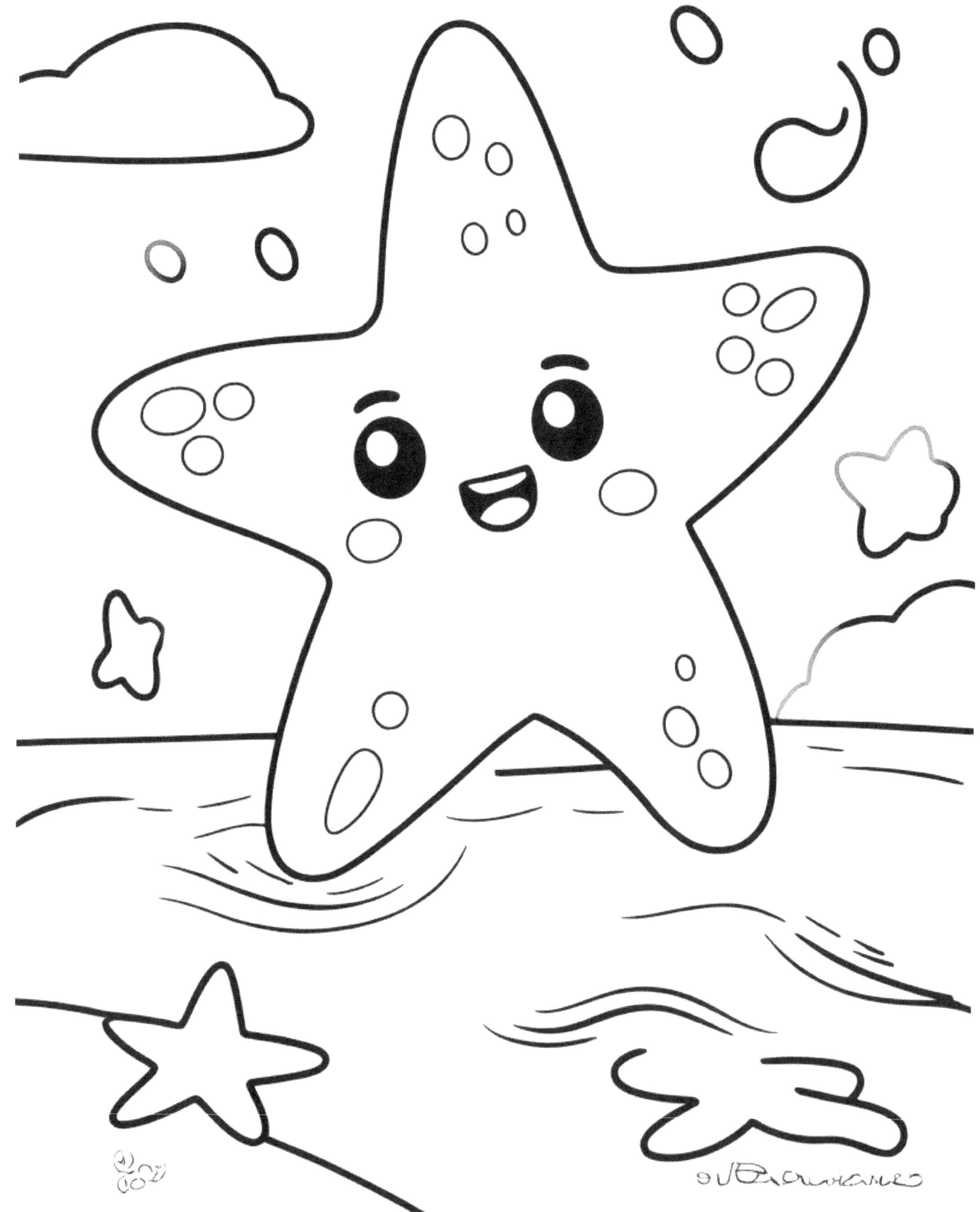

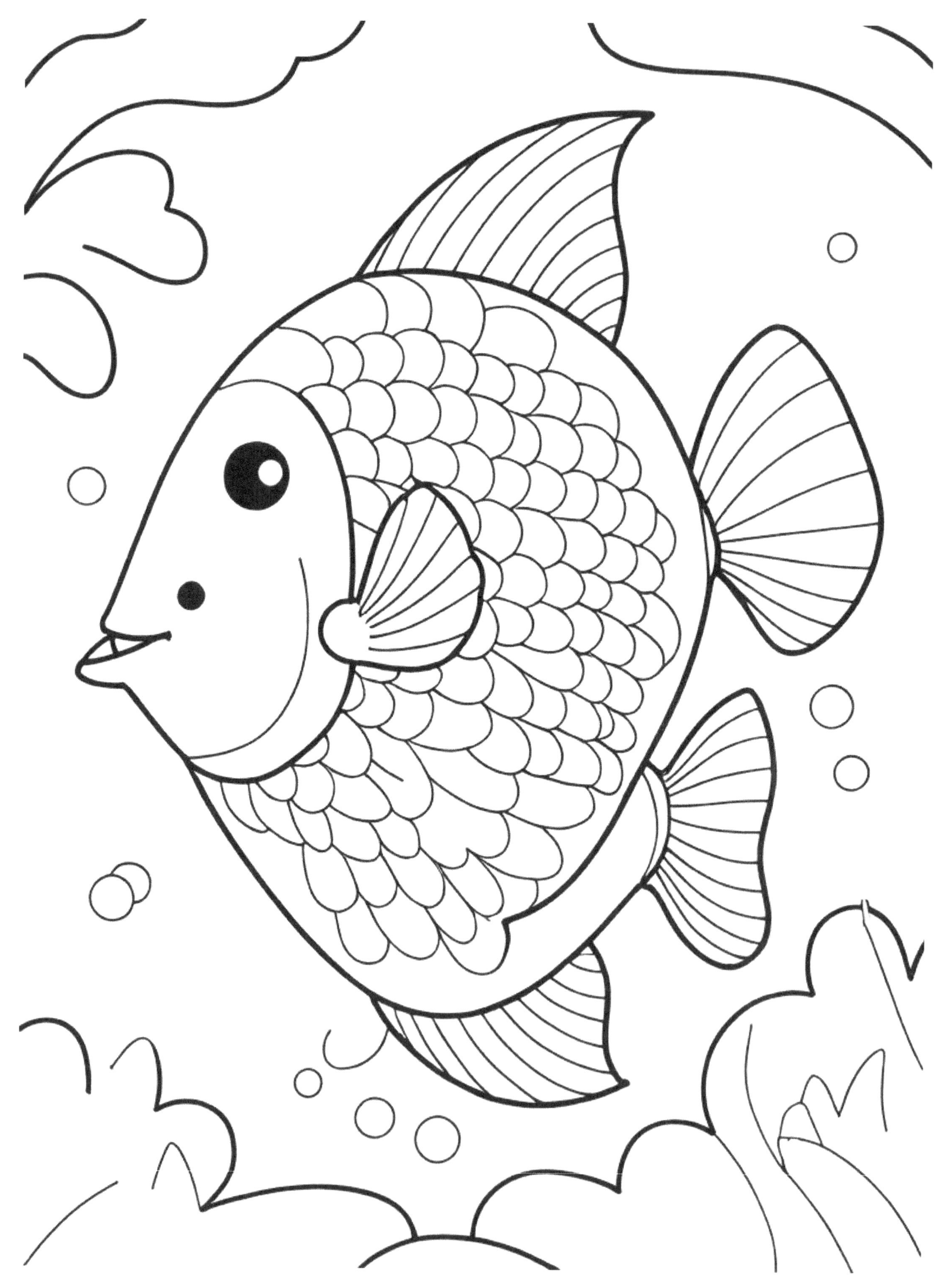

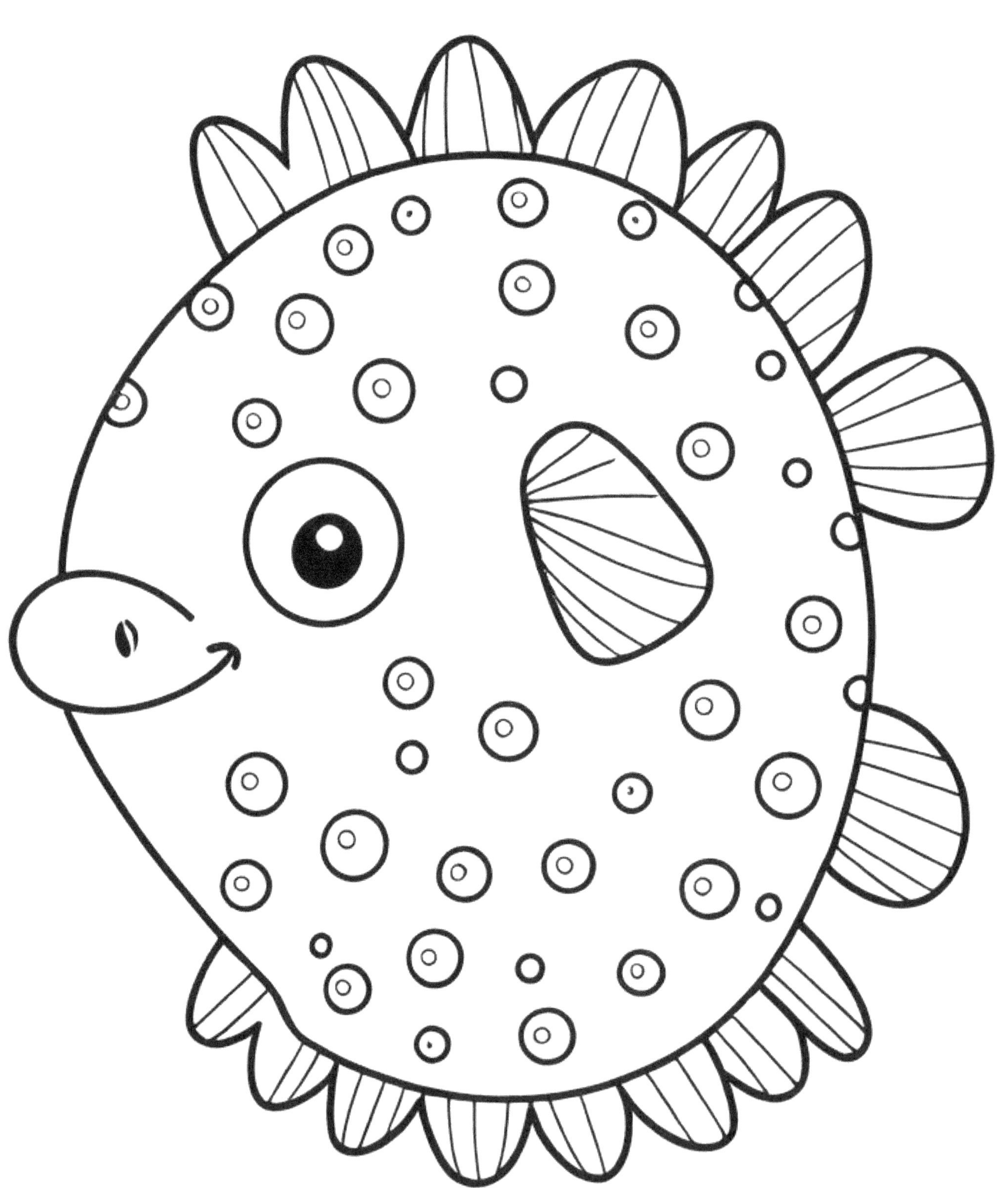

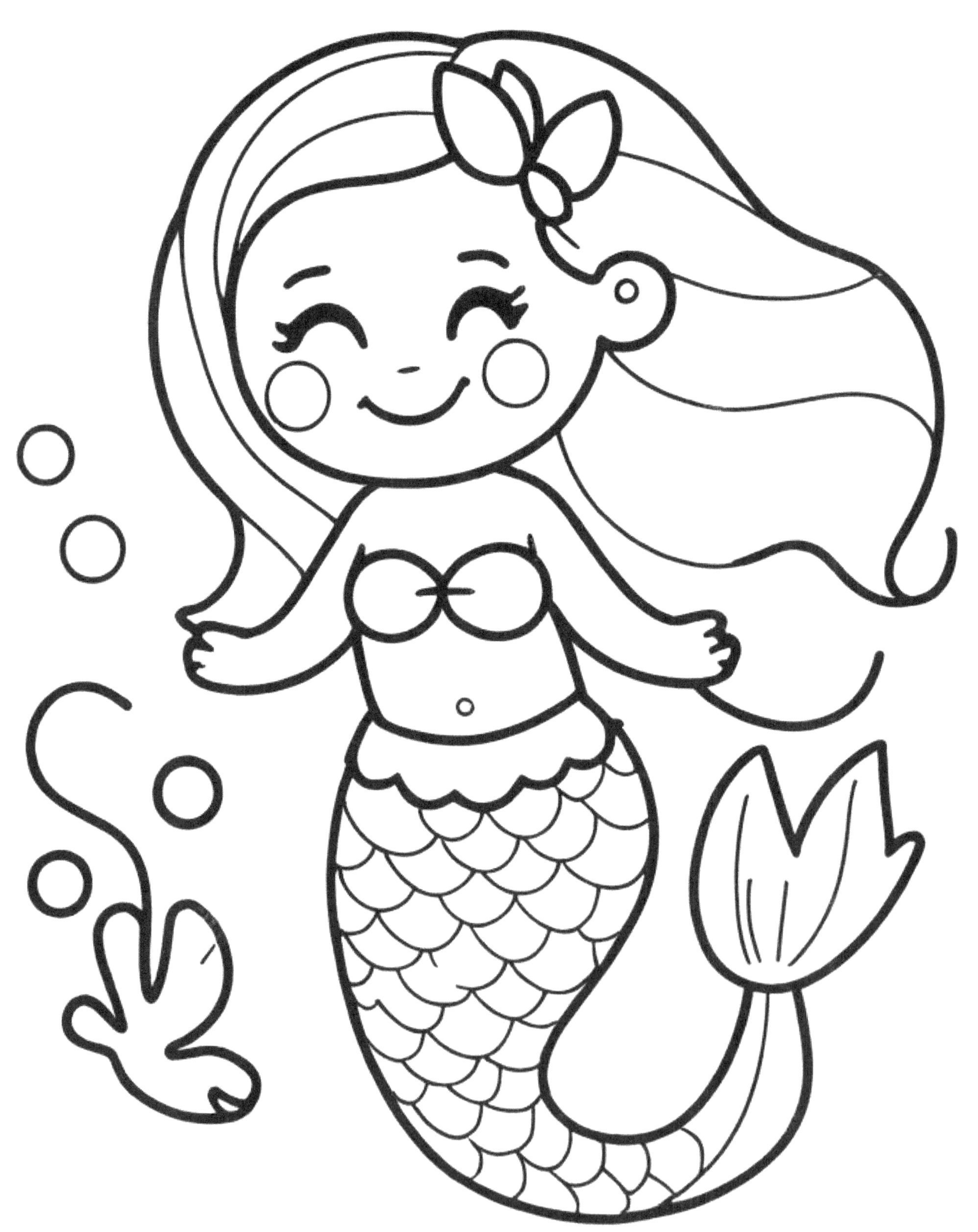

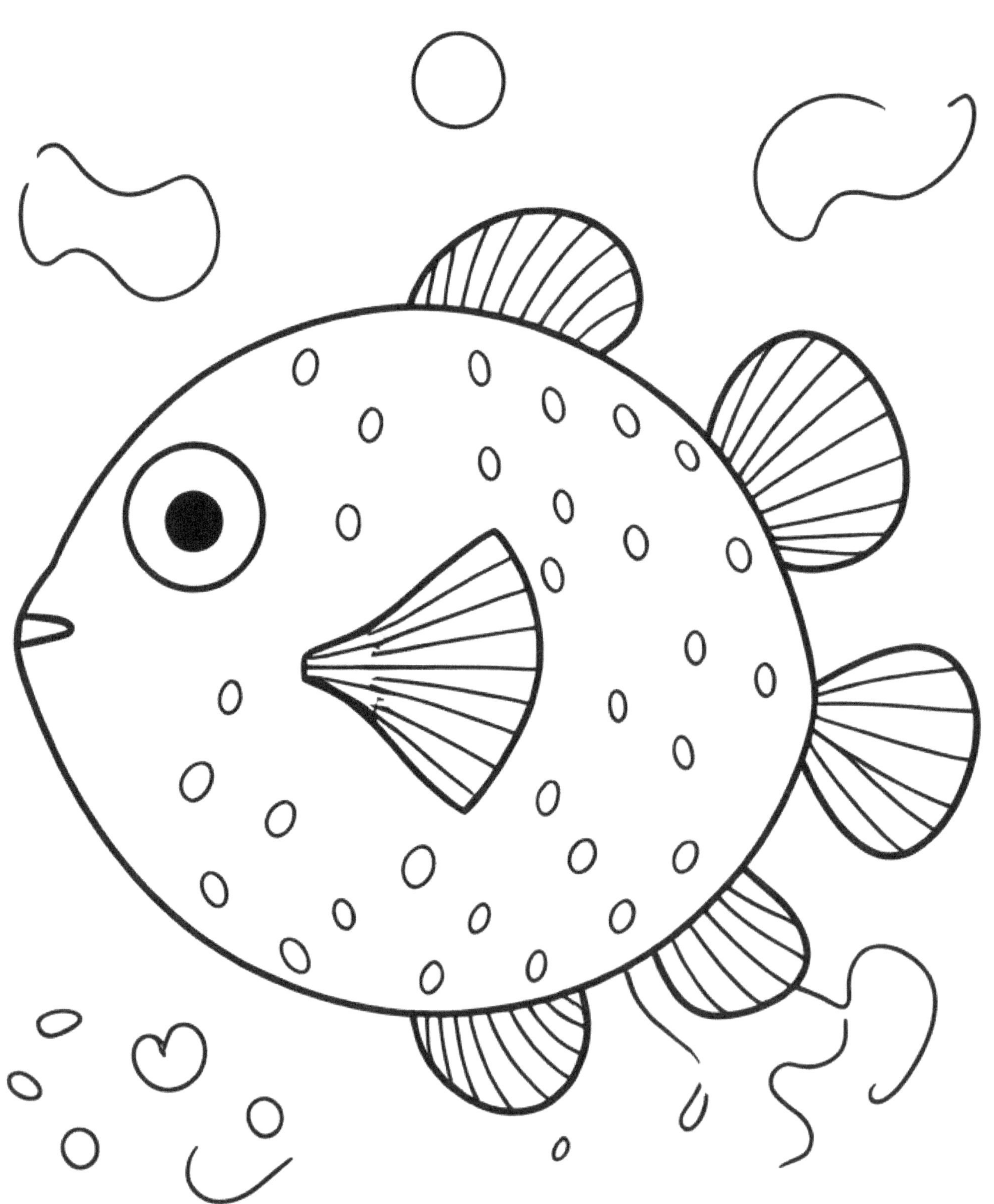

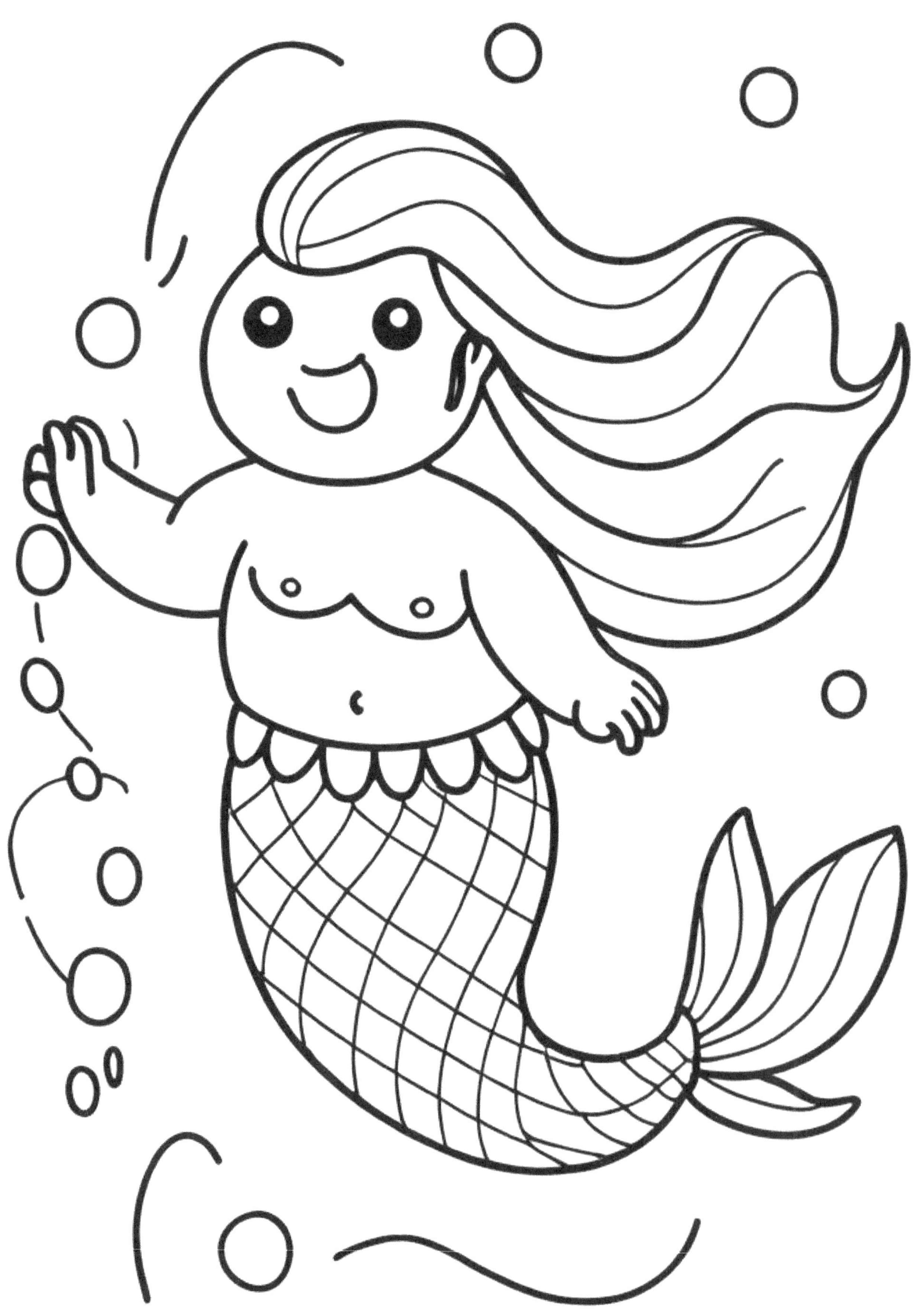

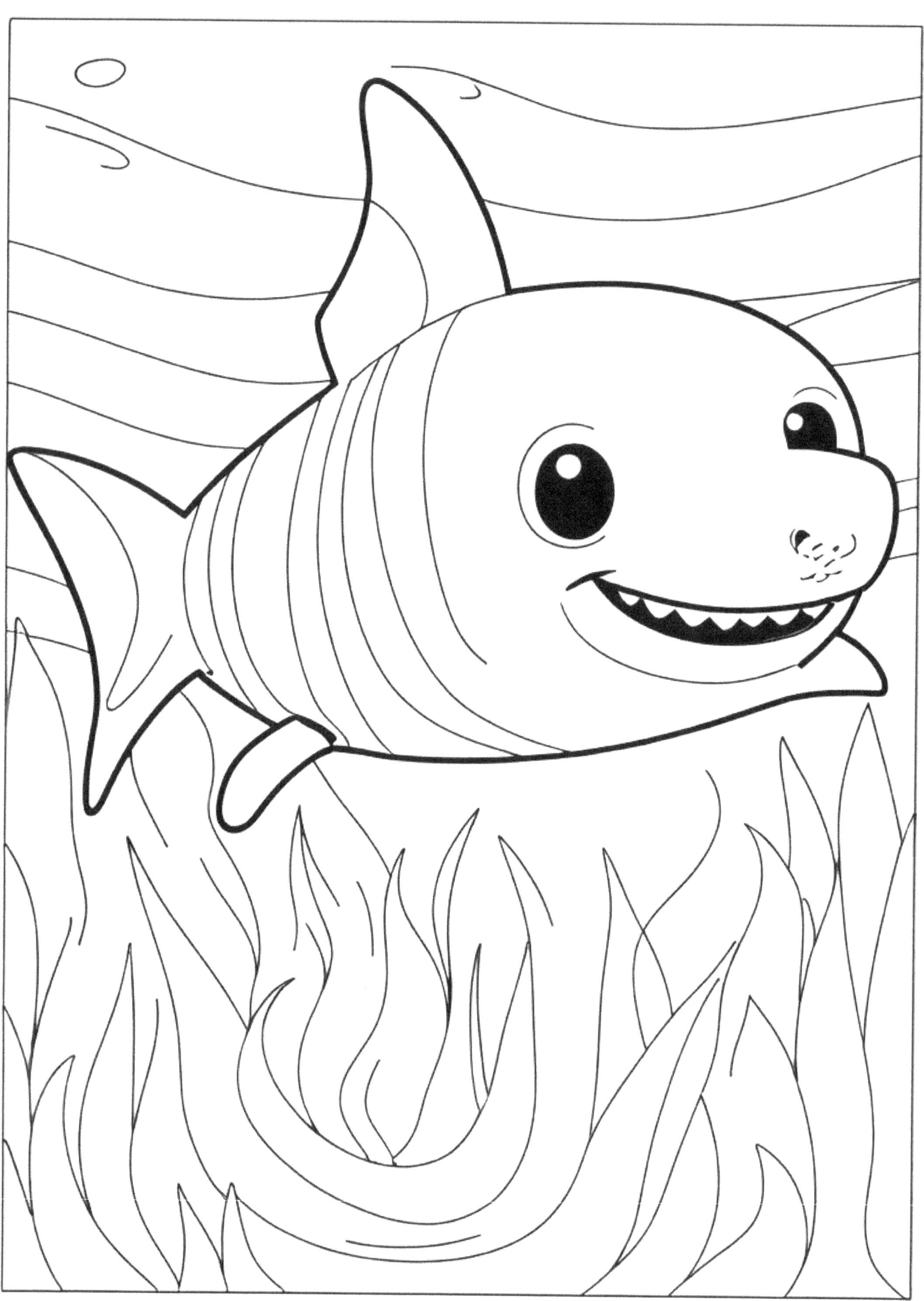